Zen
and the
Art of the
Internet

Prentice Hall Series in Innovative Technology

Dennis R. Allison, David J. Farber, and Bruce D. Shriver   *Series Advisors*

Bhasker	*A VHDL Primer*
Blachman	*Mathematica: A Practical Approach*
Chan and Mourad	*Digital Design Using Field Programmable Gate Arrays*
El-Rewini, Lewis, and Ali	*Task Scheduling in Parallel and Distributed Systems*
Johnson	*Superscalar Microprocessor Design*
Kane and Heinrich	*MIPS RISC Architecture, Second Edition*
Kehoe	*Zen and the Art of the Internet: A Beginner's Guide. Third Edition*
Lawson	*Parallel Processing in Industrial Real-Time Applications*
Nelson, ed.	*Systems Programming with Modula-e*
Nutt	*Open Systems*
Rose	*The Little Black Book: A Practical Perspective on OSI Directory Services*
Rose	*The Open Book: A Practical Perspective on OSI*
Rose	*The Simple Book: An Introduction to Management of TCP/IP-Based Internets*
Shapiro	*A C++ Toolkit*
Slater	*Microprocessor-Based Design*
SPARC International, Inc.	*The SPARC Architecture Manual, Version 8*
SPARC International, Inc.	*The SPARC Architecture Manual, Version 9*
Strom, et al.	*Hermes: A Language for Distributed Computing*
Treseler	*Designing State Machine Controllers Using Programmable Logic*
Wirfs-Brock, Wilkerson, and Weiner	*Designing Object-Oriented Software*

Zen
and the
Art of the
Internet
A Beginner's
Guide

Third Edition

Brendan P. Kehoe

PTR Prentice Hall
Englewood Cliffs, New Jersey 07632

Library of Congress Cataloging-in-Publication Data

Kehoe, Brendan P.
Zen and the art of the internet : a beginner's guide / Brendan P. Kehoe. -- 3rd ed.
    p.   cm.
Includes bibliographical references (p.   ) and index.
ISBN 0-13-121492-6
    1.Internet (Computer network)   I. Title.   II. Series.
TK5105.875.I57K44   1994   93-41531
384.3--dc20   CIP

Editorial/Production Supervision and Interior Design: Lisa Iarkowski
Interior "Globe" design: Gail Cocker-Bogusz
Acquisitions Editor: Karen Gettman
Buyer: Alexis Heydt
Cover Art: "Drum Bridge and Setting-Sun Hill" by Ando Hiroshige. Tokyo National Museum
Cover Design: Design Solutions

© 1994 PTR Prentice Hall
Prentice-Hall, Inc.
A Paramount Communications Company
Englewood Cliffs, NJ 07632

The publisher offers discounts on this book when ordered in bulk quantities.
For more information, contact:

Corporate Sales Department
PTR Prentice Hall
113 Sylvan Avenue
Englewood Cliffs, NJ 07632
Phone: 201-592-2863
FAX: 201-592-2249.

Printed in the United States of America

10 9 8 7 6 5 4 3 2 1

ISBN 0-13-083033-X

Prentice-Hall International (UK) Limited, London
Prentice-Hall of Australia Pty. Limited, Sydney
Prentice-Hall of Canada, Inc., Toronto
Prentice-Hall Hispanoamericana S.A., Mexico
Prentice-Hall of India Private Limited, New Delhi
Prentice-Hall of Japan, Inc., Tokyo
Simon & Schuster Asia Pte. Ltd., Singapore
Editora Prentice-Hall do Brasil, Ltda., Rio de Janeiro

Contents

Foreword   *xiii*

Preface   *xv*

Preface to the Second Edition   *xvii*

Acknowledgments   *xix*

1 Network Basics   *1*

Domains	2
Internet Numbers	4
Resolving Names And Numbers	4
The Networks	5
The Physical Connection	6

2 Electronic Mail   *9*

Email Addresses	9
%@!.: Symbolic Cacophony	9
Anatomy of a Mail Header	10
Bounced Mail	12
Chain Letters	13
Sending and Receiving Mail	13

Mailing Lists   15
  Listservs   16
Some Fun With Email: The Oracle   18

3 Anonymous FTP   21

FTP Etiquette   22
Basic Commands   22
  Creating the Connection   23
  dir: Directory of Files   24
  cd: Changing the Current Directory   25
  get and put: File Transfer   26
    ASCII vs. Binary, 27
    mget and mput: Multiple Files, 28
Those '.Z' Files   29
The archie *Server*   29
  Using *archie* Today   29
  archie Clients   31
  Mailing *archie*   32
  The *whatis* Database   32

4 Usenet News   35

What Usenet Is   35
The Diversity of Usenet   35
What Usenet Is Not   36
Propagation of News   38
Reading News   39
Group Creation   39
  Bogus Newsgroups   40
If You're Unhappy. . .   40

The History of Usenet (The ABCs)   *41*

Hierarchies   *43*

Moderated vs. Unmoderated   *44*

news.groups and
        news.announce.newgroups   *44*

How Usenet Works   *45*

Mail Gateways   *46*

Usenet "Netiquette"   *46*

  Signatures   *47*
  Posting Personal Messages   *47*
  Posting Mail   *48*
  Test Messages   *48*
  Famous People Appearing   *49*
  Summaries   *49*
  Quoting   *50*
  Crossposting   *50*
  A Dying Boy's Last Wish   *51*
  Recent News   *52*
  Computer Religion   *52*

Quality of Postings   *52*

  Useful Subjects   *53*
  Tone of Voice   *53*

Frequently Asked Questions   *54*

  The RTFM Archive   *54*

A Final Note   *55*

5 Telnet   *57*

Using Telnet   *57*

  Telnet Ports   *58*

Publicly Accessible Libraries   *59*

Internet Services List 60

HYTELNET 60

The Cleveland Freenet 61

Directories 62

Knowbot 62
White Pages 62

Databases and Other Resources 63

AMS E-Math 63
Colorado Alliance
    of Research Libraries (CARL) 63
Dartmouth Dante Project 64
NASA/IPAC Extragalactic
    Database 64
FEDIX—Minority Scholarship
    Information 64
Clemson University Forestry
and Agricultural Network 65
Geographic Name Server 65
Ham Radio Callbook 66
University of Maryland Info Database 66
LawNet 67
Library of Congress 67
NASA SpaceLink 67
Net Mail Sites 68
JVNCnet NICOL 68
Ocean Network Information
    Center 68
PENpages 69
Science and Technology
    Information System 69
SuperNet 70
Washington University Services 70
Weather Services 70

Bulletin Board Systems 70

6 Various Tools 75

Finger	75
Ping	77
Talk	77
Internet Navigation	78
Wide Area Information Server (WAIS)	79
The Internet Gopher	80
Veronica	82
Netfind: Finding Your Friends	83
The WHOIS Database	84
Other Uses of WHOIS	85

7 Commercial Services 87

Electronic Journals	87
ClariNet News	88
Bunyip Information Services	89
Commercial Databases	91
Online Services	91

8 Things You'll Hear About 93

The Internet Worm	93
A Coke Machine on the Internet?	95
The Cuckoo's Egg	97
Organizations	97

The Association
    for Computing Machinery   *97*
Computer Professionals
    for Social Responsibility   *98*
The Electronic Frontier Foundation   *100*
The Free Software Foundation   *101*
The Internet Society   *102*
The League
    for Programming Freedom   *103*
The Society for Electronic Access   *103*

The InterNIC   *105*

The White House   *106*

MTV on the Internet   *107*

Text Projects   *107*
    The Online Book Initiative   *108*
    Project Gutenberg   *108*

Advances in Networking   *110*
    FrEdMail   *110*
    NREN   *111*

Internet Talk Radio   *112*

Online Career Center   *114*

9 **Finding Out More**   *117*

Magazines and Newsletters   *118*
    Internet World   *118*
    Matrix News   *118*
    Internet Columns   *119*

InterNIC Directory of Directories   *120*

The NETA Diskette   *121*

The MaasInfo Package   121

John December's Internet
    CMC List   122

Requests for Comments   122

Conclusion   *125*

A Getting to Other Networks *127*

B Retrieving Files via Email   *133*

Archive Servers   133

FTP-by-Mail Servers   134

C Newsgroup Creation   *135*

Discussion   135

Voting   136

The Result of a Vote   137

Creation of the Group   138

D Items Available for FTP *139*

E Services via Telnet *147*

F Country Codes *157*

Glossary *167*

Bibliography *181*

Index *189*

Foreword

One of the wonderful things about working on the Internet is the near guarantee that help will arrive from unexpected places. In this case, a local guide prepared so that a system administrator at a small college wouldn't have to answer so many pesky questions about how to use the Net has turned out to be just the key to helping people all over the world get up to speed on the way the Internet works.

Zen and the Art of the Internet is more than just a collection of recipes of how to connect to this or that site or what arcane commands to type at what prompts. There's a lot of that, to be sure—the Net still has what John Perry Barlow terms a "savage user interface," and some amount of hand-holding is needed to guide people through the rough spots. Much more than that, though, *Zen* gives the new user of the Net some clue as

"I think, though, that if I suddenly found myself in the, to me, unthinkable position of facing a class in English usage and style, I would simply lean far out over the desk, clutch my lapels, blink my eyes, and say, 'Get the little book! Get the little book! Get the little book!'"

— E.B. White,
introduction to Strunk and White's
The Elements of Style.

to *why* things are as they are, how people interact in this environment, and an approach to make their use of the Internet less of a hunt through the wilderness.

Brendan has written a book which has been on the wish lists of network builders for a long time—a clear, straightforward, and engaging description of what the Internet is and why you want to be connected to it. While large sums of money may build bigger and faster networks, *Zen* argues that it is the mass of well trained, literate, and interesting people *behind* the wires and computers that makes them really successful.

Edward Vielmetti
Ann Arbor, MI
emv@msen.com

Preface

The Internet has come of age.

In the United States, the 1992 Presidential campaign had an unparalleled presence in Cyberspace. Candidates sported email addresses, electronically available position papers, and a heretofore unseen awareness of this "global village." In the former Soviet Union, email was one of the only ways citizens could get information out about the coup against then-President Gorbachev. And MTV is on the Net.

For those who helped build the Internet, its fantastic growth—more than doubling in size each six months—has been both exciting and sobering. Many predict that in only a few years, Internet connectivity will be available by right, in much the same way as having access to a telephone is considered a basic necessity.

To someone learning about the Net for the first time, the sheer size of it can be overwhelming. Many people feel a strong urge to panic when they first encounter the Internet, putting it on a list of things to avoid, like learning to program a VCR. I urge you to stick with it, and set your own pace. You alone control your learning process. If you need to, learn to program your VCR first, so you can tape the shows you'll miss when you're traveling through Cyberspace. Then start reading, keeping in mind that in a day or two, you'll have learned enough to actually help others use the Net.

In 1968, just before the birth of what became the Internet, J.C.R. Licklider and Robert Taylor wrote about virtual communities; a quarter of a century later, their words perfectly describe what's happened on the Net.

> *What will on-line interactive communities be like? In most fields they will consist of geographically separated members, sometimes grouped in small clusters and sometimes working individually. They will be communities not of common location but of common interest.*

And thus begins the web.

brendan@zen.org
Santa Cruz, CA

Preface to the Second Edition

Welcome to Cyberspace!

We've been expecting you. Be careful as you try out your new legs—the ground's firm, but does have some unexpected twists and turns. This book will be your guide through a vast and amazing web of new people, places, and ideas.

Zen is intended for computing novices and experienced researchers alike. It attempts to remain operating-system "neutral"—little information herein is specific to DOS, Unix, VMS, or any other environment. In its early stages, this book prompted response from a vast and disparate audience—from librarians to hobbyists to carpenters to Ph.D. physicists. It's my hope that it will be useful to nearly anyone.

Some typographical conventions are maintained throughout. All abstract items like possible filenames, usernames, etc., are represented in *italics*. Similarly, definite filenames and email addresses are represented in a quoted 'typewriter' font. A user's session is usually offset from the rest of the paragraph, as such:

```
prompt> command
        The results are usually displayed here.
```

The purpose of this book is two fold: first, it will serve as a reference piece which you can easily grab on the fly to look something up. You'll also gain a foundation from which you can explore your surroundings at your leisure. *Zen and the Art of the Internet* doesn't spend a significant amount of time on any one point; rather, it provides enough for people to learn the specifics of what his or her local system offers.

One warning is perhaps in order—this territory we are entering can become a fantastic time-sink. Hours can slip by, people can come and go, and you'll be locked in Cyberspace. Remember to do your work!

With that, it's my distinct pleasure to usher you into the Net.

brendan@zen.org
Chester, PA

Acknowledgments

Certain sections in this booklet are not my original work—rather, they are derived from documents that were available on the Internet and already aptly stated their areas of concentration. The chapter on Usenet is, in large part, made up of what is posted monthly to news.announce.newusers, with some editing and rewriting. Also, the main section on *archie* was derived from 'whatis.archie' by Peter Deutsch, then of the McGill University Computing Centre. It's available via anonymous FTP from archie.mcgill.ca. Much of what's in the telnet section came from an impressive introductory document put together by SuraNet, along with a few discoveries from Scott Yanoff's list. Some definitions in the glossary are from an excellent one put together by Colorado State University.

It would be remiss of me not to thank those who provided the moral and inspirational support that has been so invaluable throughout this whole process: Sven Heinicke, at whose house I wrote a good 40% of the first edition of the guide over a Christmas break; Jennifer Kowaleuski; Chip Page; and Patrick Quairoli, for his grace under pressure. And my thanks to Jeffrey Osier, for all of his help and great music. I'm proud to call them my friends.

Zen would not be the same without the aid of many people on the Net, and the providers of resources that are already out there. Many, many people sent in encouraging notes and a few corrections for mistakes or changes in the second edition. I'd also like to thank the folks who provided much-needed information on the fly, or gave comments, suggestions, and criticisms to early drafts of the guide and its parts: Andy Blankenbiller, Vint Cerf, Alan Emtage, Brian Fitzgerald, John Goetsch, Jeff Kellem, Bill Krauss, Steve Lodin, Mike Nesel, Bob Neveln, Wanda Pierce, Joshua Poulson, Dave Sill, Bob Smart, Gene Spafford, Ed Vielmetti, Craig Ward, and Chip Yamasaki. Glee Willis of the University of Nevada-Reno deserves particular mention for all of her work—this guide would have been considerably less polished without her help.

Finally, mixed thanks to Anne Rice, whose books *The Witching Hour* and *Lasher* were absolutely fantastic. I got so hooked that I ended up just barely meeting my deadline.

1 Network Basics

We are truly in an information society. Now more than ever, moving vast amounts of information quickly across great distances is one of our most pressing needs. From small one-person entrepreneurial efforts to the largest of corporations, more and more professional people are discovering that the only way to be successful in the '90s and beyond is to realize that technology is advancing at a break-neck pace—and they must somehow keep up. Likewise, researchers from all corners of the earth are finding that their work thrives in a networked environment. Immediate access to the work of colleagues and a "virtual" library of millions of volumes and thousands of papers affords them the ability to incorporate a body of knowledge heretofore unthinkable. Work groups can now conduct interactive conferences with each other, paying no heed to physical location—the possibilities are endless.

You have at your fingertips the ability to talk in "real time" with someone in Japan, send a 2,000-word short story to a group of people who will critique it for the sheer pleasure of doing so, see if a Macintosh sitting in a lab in Canada is turned on, and find out if someone happens to be sitting in front of their computer (*logged on*) in Australia, all inside of thirty minutes. No airline (or Tardis, for that matter) could ever match that travel itinerary.

The largest problem people face when first using a network is grasping all that's available. Even seasoned users find themselves surprised when they discover a new service or feature that they'd never known even existed. Once acquainted with the terminology and sufficiently comfort-

1

able with making occasional mistakes, the learning process will drastically speed up.

Domains

 Getting where you want to go can often be one of the more difficult aspects of using networks. The variety of ways in which places are named will probably leave a blank stare on your face at first. Don't fret; there is a method to this apparent madness.

If someone were to ask for a home address, they would probably expect a street, apartment, city, state, and zip code. That's all the information the post office needs to deliver mail in a reasonably speedy fashion. Likewise, computer addresses have a structure to them. The general form is:

a person's email address on a computer: user@somewhere.domain
a computer's name: somewhere.domain

The *user* portion is usually the person's account name on the system, though it doesn't have to be: somewhere.domain tells you the name of a system or location, and what kind of organization it is. The trailing *domain* is often one of the following:

com	Usually a company or other commercial institution or organization, like Convex Computers (convex.com).
edu	An educational institution, for example, New York University, named nyu.edu.
gov	A government site; for example, NASA is nasa.gov.
mil	A military site, like the Air Force (af.mil).
net	Gateways and other administrative hosts for a network (it does not mean all of the hosts in a network). nic.near.net and nic.eu.net are examples of these kinds of gateways.

| org | This is a domain reserved for private organizations, that don't comfortably fit in the other classes of domains. One example is the Electronic Frontier Foundation, named eff.org. |

Each individual country also has its own top-level domain. For example, the us domain includes each of the fifty states (but is usually only used for small sites). Other countries represented with domains include:

au	Australia
ca	Canada
fr	France
uk	The United Kingdom. These also have sub-domains separated by type; for example, ac.uk is used for academic sites and co.uk for commercial ones.

See Appendix F, *Country Codes*, for a full listing of the country domains.

The proper terminology for a site's domain name (*somewhere.domain* above) is its *Fully Qualified Domain Name*, or FQDN. It is usually selected to give a clear indication of the site's organization or sponsoring agent. For example, the Massachusetts Institute of Technology's FQDN is mit.edu; likewise, Apple Computer's domain name is apple.com. While such obvious names are usually the norm, there are the occasional exceptions that are ambiguous enough to mislead—like vt.edu, which, on first impulse, one might surmise is an educational institution of some sort in Vermont; not so. It's actually the domain name for Virginia Tech. In most cases it's relatively easy to glean the meaning of a domain name—such confusion is far from the norm.

Internet Numbers

 Every single machine on the Internet has a unique address,[1] called its *Internet number* or *IP Address*. It's actually a 32-bit number, but is most commonly represented as four numbers joined by periods ('.'), like 147.31.254.130. This is sometimes also called a *dotted quad*; there are literally thousands of different possible dotted quads. The ARPAnet (the mother of today's Internet) originally only had the capacity to have up to 256 systems on it because of the way each system was addressed. In the early '80s, it became clear that things would fast outgrow such a small limit; the 32-bit addressing method was born, freeing thousands of host numbers. However, there is growing concern that there may be a shortfall of addresses by the end of the twentieth century.

Each piece of an Internet address (like 192) is called an *octet*, representing one of four sets of eight bits. The first two or three pieces (say 192.55.239) represent the network that a system is on, called its *subnet*. For example, all of the computers for Wesleyan University are in the subnet 129.133. They can have numbers like 129.133.10.10 and 129.133.230.19, up to 65,000 possible combinations (possible computers).

IP addresses and domain names aren't assigned arbitrarily—that would lead to unbelievable confusion. An application must be filed with the InterNIC Registration Services, either electronically, by sending mail to hostmaster@rs.internic.net, or via regular mail.

Resolving Names and Numbers

 OK, computers can be referred to by either their FQDN or their Internet address. How can one user be expected to remember all of those names?

They're not. The Internet is designed so that one can use either method. Since humans find it much more natural to

---

1. At least one address, possibly two or even three—but we won't go into that.

deal with words than numbers, in most cases the FQDN for each host is mapped to its Internet number. Each domain is *served* by a computer within that domain, which provides all of the necessary information to go from a domain name to an IP address, and vice-versa. For example, when someone refers to foosun.bar.com, the *resolver* knows that it should ask a certain system, say foovax.bar.com, about systems in the bar.com domain. If the name foosun.bar.com really exists, foovax will send foosun's Internet address to the system that used it. All of this "magic" happens behind the scenes.

Rarely will a user have to remember the Internet number of a site. However, you will remember a substantial number of FQDNs. It will eventually reach a point when you are able to make a reasonably accurate guess at what domain name a certain college, university, or company might have, given just their name.

The Networks

 Internet

The Internet is a large "network of networks." There is no one network known as The Internet; rather, regional nets like SuraNet, PrepNet, NearNet, et al. are all interconnected (nay, "internetworked") together into one great living thing, communicating at amazing speeds with the TCP/IP protocol. All activity takes place in "realtime." The Internet offers mail, file transfer, remote login, and a plethora of other services.

➡ *UUCP*

The UUCP network is a loose association of systems all communicating with the UUCP protocol. (UUCP stands for 'Unix-to-Unix Copy Program'.) It's based on two systems (e.g., *oregano* and *basil*) connecting to each other at specified intervals, called *polling*, and executing any work scheduled for either of them. Historically, most UUCP was done with Unix equipment, although the software's since been implemented on other platforms (including VMS and DOS).

Let's say the system *oregano* polls the system *basil* once every two hours. If there's any mail waiting for *oregano*, *basil* will send it at that time; likewise, *oregano* will at that time send any jobs waiting for *basil*. Mail and Usenet news are the primary offerings of UUCP, although some general file transfer is available with the proper permission.

➡ BITNET

BITNET (the "Because It's Time Network") is comprised of systems connected by *point-to-point* links, all running the NJE protocol. It's continued to grow, but has found itself suffering at the hands of the falling costs of Internet connections. Also, a number of mail gateways are in place to reach users on other networks. BITNET offers mail, mailing lists, and some file transfer, but cannot support remote login. It is possible, though, to have interactive "discussions" with people on other machines. BITNET supports the ability to send a line of up to 160 characters to any user on any system.

The Physical Connection

The actual connections between the various networks take a variety of forms. The most common for Internet links are *56k leased lines* (dedicated telephone lines carrying 56 kilobit-per-second connections) and T1 lines (special) phone lines with 1 million bit-per-second connections). Also installed are *T3 links*, acting as backbones between major locations to carry a massive load of traffic: 45 million bits per second. All of these numbers are rarely of concern to the typical user—things will just go very, very fast.

These links are paid for by each institution to a local carrier. Also available are *SLIP* connections, which carry Internet traffic (packets) over high-speed modems.

UUCP links are made with modems (for the most part), that run from 1200 baud all the way up to as high as 38.4 Kbps. As was mentioned previously, the connections are of the *store-and-forward* variety.

Also in use are Internet-based UUCP links. (As if things weren't already confusing enough!) The systems do their UUCP traffic over TCP/IP connections, which give the UUCP-based network some blindingly fast "hops," resulting in better connectivity for the network as a whole. UUCP connections first became popular in the 1970s, and have remained in widespread use ever since.

BITNET links mostly take the form of 9600-bps modems connected from site to site. Often places have three or more links going; the majority, however, look to "upstream" sites for their sole link to the network.

"The Glory and the Nothing of a Name"

— Byron, "Churchill's Grave"

2 Electronic Mail

The desire to communicate is the essence of networking. People have always wanted to correspond with each other in the fastest way possible, short of normal conversation. Electronic mail (or *email*) is the most prevalent application of this in computer networking. It allows people to write back and forth without having to spend much time worrying about how the message actually gets delivered. As technology grows closer and closer to being a common part of daily life, the need to understand the many ways it can be utilized and how it works, at least to some level, is vital.

Email Addresses

Electronic mail is hinged around the concept of an *address*; the previous chapter made some reference to it while introducing domains. Your *email address* provides all of the information required to get a message to you from anywhere in the world.

An address doesn't necessarily have to go to a human being. It could be an archive server,[1] a list of people, or even someone's pocket pager. These cases are the exception to the norm—mail to most addresses is read by human beings.

%@!.: Symbolic Cacophony

Email addresses usually appear in one of two forms—either in Internet format, which uses an "at" sign (the '@' symbol), or in UUCP format,

---

1. See Appendix B, *Retrieving Files via Email,* to learn about archive servers.

9

which uses an exclamation point (the '!' symbol), which is sometimes referred to as a "bang". The latter of the two, UUCP "bang" paths, tend to be more restrictive, yet more clearly dictate how the mail will travel.

To reach Jim Morrison on the system south.america.org, one would address the mail as 'jm@south.america.org'. But if Jim's account was on a UUCP site named *brazil*, then his address would be 'brazil!jm'. If it's possible (and one exists), try to use the Internet form of an address; bang paths can fail if an intermediate site in the path happens to be down. There is a growing trend for UUCP sites to register Internet domain names to help alleviate the problem of path failures.

Another symbol that enters the fray is '%'—it acts as an extra "routing" method. For example, if the UUCP site dream is connected to south.america.org but doesn't have an Internet domain name of its own, a user named debbie on dream might be reached by writing to the address

debbie%dream@south.america.org

The form is significant. This address says that the local system should first send the mail to south.america.org. There the address debbie%dream will turn into debbie@dream, which will hopefully be a valid address. Then south.america.org will handle getting the mail to the host dream, where it will be delivered locally to debbie.

Many of the intricacies of email addressing methods are fully covered in the book *!%@:: A Directory of Electronic Mail Addressing and Networks*, published by O'Reilly and Associates as part of their Nutshell Handbook series. It is a must for any active email user. Write to 'nuts@ora.com' for ordering information.

Anatomy of a Mail Header

An electronic mail message has a specific structure to it that's common across every type of computer system.[2] A possible message might be:

2. The standard is written down in RFC-822. See page 122 for more info on how to get copies of the various RFCs.

```
From bush@hq.mil Sat May 25 17:06:01 1991
Received: from hq.mil by house.gov with SMTP id AA21901
   (4.1/SMI for dan@house.gov); Sat, 25 May 91 17:05:56 -0400
Date: Sat, 25 May 91 17:05:56 -0400
From: The President <bush@hq.mil>
Message-Id: <9105252105.AA06631@hq.mil>
To: dan@senate.gov
Subject: Meeting


Hi Dan .. we have a meeting at 9:30 a.m. with the Joint Chiefs. Please don't
oversleep this time.
```

The first line, with 'From' and the two lines for 'Received:', are usually not very interesting. They give the "real" address that the mail is coming from (as opposed to the address you should reply to, which may look much different), and what places the mail went through to get to you. Over the Internet, there is always at least one 'Received:' header and usually no more than four or five. When a message is sent using UUCP, one 'Received:' header is added for each system that the mail passes through. This can often result in more than a dozen 'Received:' headers. While they help with dissecting problems in mail delivery, odds are that the average user will never want to see them. Most mail programs will filter out this kind of "cruft" in a header.

The 'Date:' header contains the date and time the message was sent. Likewise, the "good" address (as opposed to "real" address) is laid out in the 'From:' header. Sometimes it won't include the full name of the person (in this case, 'The President'), and may look different, but it should always contain an email address of some form.

The message ID of a message is intended mainly for tracing mail routing and is rarely of interest to normal users. Every message ID is guaranteed to be unique.

'To:' lists the email address (or addresses) of the recipients of the message. There may be a 'Cc:' header, listing additional addresses. Finally, a brief subject for the message goes in the 'Subject:' header.

The exact order of a message's headers may vary from system to system, but it will always include these fundamental headers, which are vital to proper delivery.

Bounced Mail

When an email address is incorrect in some way (the system's name is wrong, the domain doesn't exist, whatever), the mail system will *bounce* the message back to the sender, much the same way that the Postal Service does when you send a letter to a bad street address. The message will include the reason for the bounce; a common error is addressing mail to an account name that doesn't exist. For example, writing to Lisa Simpson at Widener University's Computer Science department will fail, because she doesn't have an account.[3]

```
From: Mail Delivery Subsystem <MAILER-DAEMON>
Date: Sat, 25 May 91 16:45:14 -0400
To: mg@gracie.com (Matt Groening)
Cc: Postmaster@cs.widener.edu
Subject: Returned mail: User unknown

    ----- Transcript of session follows -----
While talking to cs.widener.edu:
>>> RCPT To:<lsimpson@cs.widener.edu>
<<< 550 <lsimpson@cs.widener.edu>... User unknown
550 lsimpson... User unknown
```

As you can see, a carbon copy of the message (the 'Cc:' header entry) was sent to the postmaster of Widener's CS department. The *Postmaster* is responsible for maintaining a reliable mail system on his system or network. Usually, postmasters at sites will attempt to aid you in getting your mail where it's supposed to go. If a typing error was made, try resending the message. If you're sure that the address is correct, contact the postmaster of the site directly and ask him for help in reaching the user.

The message also includes the text of the mail, so you don't have to retype everything you wrote.

---

3. Though if she asked, we'd certainly give her one.

```
----- Unsent message follows -----
Received: by cs.widener.edu id AA06528; Sat, 25 May 91    16:45:14 -0400
Date: Sat, 25 May 91 16:45:14 -0400
From: Matt Groening <mg@gracie.com>
Message-Id: <9105252045.AA06528@gracie.com>
To: lsimpson@cs.widener.edu
Subject: Scripting your future episodes
Reply-To: writing-group@gracie.com

   . . . verbiage . . .
```

The body of the message can be cut out with an editor and fed right back into the mail system with a proper address, making redelivery a relatively painless process.

Chain Letters

In "real" life, a chain letter is one that promises good fortune if you copy and send a letter to some number of other people. People create email chain letters as well. They tend to cause nothing but damage to systems that are involved in them. If a chain letter is sent to five people, and those five people each send it on to another five people, more than six hundred mail messages can be generated in less than an hour. Followed through, in one day a chain letter could generate over sixty thousand email messages. The effect of this kind of explosive traffic on a system which is intimately involved in it (e.g., many of the people resending the letters send them to friends at school) can lead to disaster.

Indeed, MIT experienced just that—their main mail gateway was down for a period of time because students were repeatedly sending chain letters around. The problems caused by email chain letters cannot be emphasized enough: if you receive a chain letter, immediately report it to the postmaster of the system it came from. They stop being fun when no one at a site can receive mail because the mail queues are clogged.

Sending and Receiving Mail

We'll make one quick diversion from being OS-neuter here, to show you what it will look like to send and receive a mail message on a Unix

Calvin and **Hobbes**

system. There are *many* different mail programs for Unix alone, not to mention VMS and other systems. Check with your system administrator for specific instructions related to mail at your site.

A person sending mail would probably do something like this:

```
% mail sven@cs.widener.edu
Subject: print job's stuck

I typed `print babe.gif' and it didn't work! Why??
```

The next time Sven checked his mail, he would see it listed as:

```
% mail
"/usr/spool/mail/sven": 1 messages 1 new 1 unread
 U 1 joeuser@foo.widene Tue May 5 20:36 29/956 print job's stuck
?
```

which gives information on the sender of the email, when it was sent, and the subject of the message. He would probably use the reply command of Unix mail to send this response:

```
? r
To: joeuser@foo.wide ier.edu
Subject: Re: print job's stuck

You shouldn't print binary files like GIFs to a printer!

Ciao.
```

by Bill Watterson

Try sending yourself mail a few times to get used to your system's mailer. It'll save a lot of wasted aspirin for both you and those who may be paid to help you.

Mailing Lists

People who share common interests are inclined to discuss their hobby or interest at every available opportunity. One modern way to aid in this exchange of information is by using a *mailing list*—an email address that redistributes all mail sent to it back out to a list of addresses. For example, the Sun Managers mailing list (of interest to people that administer computers manufactured by Sun Microsystems) has the address 'sun-managers@eecs.nwu.edu'. Any mail sent to that address will "explode" out to each person named in a file maintained on a computer at Northwestern University.

Administrative tasks (sometimes referred to as *administrivia*) are often handled through other addresses, typically with the suffix '-request'. To continue the above, a request to be added to or deleted from the Sun Managers list should be sent to 'sun-managers-request@eecs.nwu.edu'.

When in doubt, try to write to the '-request' version of a mailing list address first; the other people on the list aren't interested in your desire to be added or deleted, and can certainly do nothing to expedite your request. Often, if the administrator of a list is busy (remember, this is all peripheral to real jobs and real work), many users find it necessary to ask again and again, often with harsher and harsher language, to be removed from a list. This does nothing more than waste traffic and bother everyone else receiving the messages. If, after a reasonable amount of time, you still haven't succeeded in being removed from a mailing list, write to the postmaster at that site and see if they can help.

Exercise caution when replying to a message sent by a mailing list. If you wish to respond to the author only, make *sure* that the only address you're replying to is that person, and not the entire list. Often messages such as "Yes, I agree with you completely!" will appear on a list, boring the daylights out of the other readers. Likewise, if you explicitly do want to send the message to the whole list, you'll save yourself some time by checking to make sure it's indeed headed to the whole list and not to a single person.

A list of the currently available mailing lists is available in at least two places; the first is the *List of Lists* on ftp.nisc.sri.com in the '/netinfo' directory as 'interest-groups'. It's updated fairly regularly, but is large (presently around 700K), so only get it every once in a while. To be notified as new mailing lists are added, write to 'interest-groups-request@nisc.sri.com'.

The other list, which is maintained by Gene Spafford, (spaf@cs.purdue.edu), is posted in parts to the newsgroup news.lists semi-regularly. (See Chapter 4, *Usenet News*, for info on how to read this and other newsgroups.)

Listservs

On BITNET there's an automated system for maintaining discussion lists called the *listserv*. Rather than have an already harried and overworked human take care of additions and removals from a list, a program performs these and other tasks by responding to a set of user-driven commands.

Areas of interest are wide and varied—SF-LOVERS deals with fantasy and science fiction, while ADND-L has to do with a well-known role-playing game. A full list of the available BITNET lists can be obtained by writing to 'LISTSERV@BITNIC.BITNET' with a body containing the command

list global

However, be sparing in your use of this—find out if it's already on your system somewhere. The reply is quite large.

The most fundamental command is 'subscribe'. It will tell the listserv to add the sender to a specific list. The usage is

subscribe foo-l *Your Real Name*

It will respond with a message saying either that you've been added to the list, or that the request has been passed on to the system on which the list is actually maintained.

To remove your address from a BITNET list, send the listserv

signoff foo-l

You will receive notification of your removal. If he or she is so inclined, the maintainer of the list may write you to ask if there's anything that displeased you about the mailing list that spurred your decision to leave it.

If you decide to leave *every* list, you can use the command

signoff global

This can be handy if your account is going to be turned off, or if you discover it's interfering with your work. For a full list of the available listserv commands, write to 'LISTSERV@BITNIC.BITNET', giving it the command 'help'.

American University maintains a *gateway* of every BITNET listserv list into the Usenet hierarchy 'bit.listserv'. For example, SF-LOVERS is available as the Usenet newsgroup bit.listserv.ethics-l.

As an aside, there have been implementations of the listserv system for non-BITNET hosts (more specifically, Unix systems). One of the most complete is available on cs.bu.edu in the directory pub/listserv; it provides the functionality of its BITNET counterpart without much of the often confusing complexity.

Some Fun With Email: The Oracle

 Steve Kinzler of Indiana University and Ray Moody, then of Purdue University, created a truly novel utility on the Net: the Usenet Oracle. Despite its name, the Oracle doesn't have much to do with Usenet (aside from being gatewayed into the group rec.humor.oracle in the form of the *Usenet Oracularities*).[4]

You can use the Oracle by writing to the following address: 'oracle@cs.indiana.edu'. If you'd like lots of information about the Oracle, including historical background on the ancient Oracle of Delphi, send your mail with a 'Subject:' line containing the word 'help'.

To ask the Oracle a question, your 'Subject:' line should contain the phrase "tell me". For example, a typical question might look like the following; be as creative as you can.

```
To: oracle@cs.indiana.edu
Subject: Oracle Most Wise, please tell me ...


O Wise Oracle, whose party gags are always funny, even if they involve lamp-
shades, and whose pickup lines are always successful, even if they involve the
zodiac, please enlighten your supplicant on the following:

What is the best pickup line in history?
```

As you can see, the Oracle is not intended to be used for serious questions. Embellishment before you ask your question can help make it even more entertaining.

4. See the next chapter, *Usenet News*, to learn about Usenet.

In answer, you will receive a message with a response from the Oracle. As "payment" for the privilege of using the Oracle, you may be asked to answer someone else's question.

For the question above, the Oracle might respond with

```
Date: Mon, 06 Sep 93 10:08:24 -0500
From: Usenet Oracle <oracle@cs.indiana.edu>

The Usenet Oracle has pondered your question deeply.
Your question was:

> O Wise Oracle, . . .
>
> What is the best pickup line in history?

And in response, thus spoke the Oracle:

} The best pickup line in history is, of course, FORD.
}
} You owe the Oracle one 1993 Ford F350 with all the extras.
```

Getting the jokes in the Oracle's replies is left as an exercise for the reader.

"I made this letter longer than usual because I lack the time to make it shorter."

— Pascal, *Provincial Letters XVI*

3 Anonymous FTP

FTP (the *File Transfer Protocol*) is the primary method of transferring files over the Internet. On many systems, it's also the name of the program that implements the protocol. Given proper permission, it's possible to copy a file from a computer in South Africa to one in Los Angeles at very fast speeds (on the order of 5-10K per second). This normally requires either a user ID on both systems or a special configuration set up by the system administrator(s).

There is a good way around this restriction—the *anonymous FTP* service. It essentially will let anyone in the world have access to a certain area of disk space in a nonthreatening way. With this, people can make files publicly available with little hassle. Some systems have dedicated entire disks or even entire computers to maintaining extensive archives of source code and information. They include ftp.uu.net (UUNET), wuarchive.wustl.edu (Washington University in Saint Louis), and archive.cis.ohio-state.edu (The Ohio State University).

The process involves the "foreign" user (someone not on the system itself) creating an FTP connection and logging into the system as the user 'anonymous', with an arbitrary password:

```
Name (foo.site.com:you): anonymous
Password: jm@south.america.org
```

Custom and "netiquette" dictate that people respond to the Password: query with an email address so that the sites can track the level of FTP usage, if they desire. (See page 9 for information on email addresses.)

21

The speed of the transfer depends on the speed of the underlying link. A site that has a 9600bps SLIP connection will not get the same throughput as a system with a 56k leased line. (See page 6 for more information on what kinds of connections can exist in a network.) Also, the traffic of all other users on that link will affect performance. If there are 30 people all FTPing from one site simultaneously, the load on the system (in addition to the network connection) will degrade the overall throughput of the transfer.

FTP Etiquette

Lest we forget, the Internet is there for people to do their work. People using the network and the systems on it are doing so for a purpose, whether it be research, development, or whatever. Any heavy activity takes away from the overall performance of the network as a whole.

The effects of an FTP connection on a site and its link can vary; the general rule of thumb is that any extra traffic created detracts from the ability of that site's users to perform their tasks. To be considerate of this, it's *highly* recommended that FTP sessions be held only after normal business hours for that site, preferably late at night. The possible effects of a large transfer will be less destructive at 2 a.m. than at 2 p.m. Also, remember that if it's past dinnertime in Maine, it's still early afternoon in California— think in terms of the current time at the site that's being visited, not local time.

Basic Commands

While there have been many extensions to the various FTP clients out there, there is a *de facto* "standard" set that everyone expects to work. For more information, read the manual for your FTP program. This section will only skim the bare minimum of commands needed to op-erate an FTP session.

Creating the Connection

The actual command to use FTP will vary among operating systems; for the sake of clarity, we'll use 'ftp' here, since it's the most common.

There are two ways to connect to a system—using its *hostname* or its Internet number. Using the hostname is usually preferred. However, some sites aren't able to *resolve* hostnames properly, and have no alternative. We'll assume you're able to use hostnames, for simplicity's sake. Contact your local administrator or support staff for tips on getting around any local restrictions or problems.

The form of the command is:

```
ftp somewhere.domain
```

See page 2 for help with reading and using domain names (in the example below, *somewhere.domain* is ftp.uu.net).

You must first know the name of the system you want to connect to. We'll use ftp.uu.net as an example. On your system, type:

```
ftp ftp.uu.net
```

(The actual syntax will vary depending on the type of system the connection's being made from.) It will pause momentarily, then respond with the message

```
Connected to ftp.uu.net.
```

and an initial prompt will appear:

```
220 uunet FTP server (Version 5.100 Mon Feb 11 17:13:28 EST   1991) ready.
Name (ftp.uu.net:jm):
```

to which you should respond with anonymous:

```
220 uunet FTP server (Version 5.100 Mon Feb 11 17:13:28 EST   1991) ready.
Name (ftp.uu.net:jm): anonymous
```

The system will then prompt you for a password; as noted previously, a good response is your email address:

```
331 Guest login ok, send ident as password.
Password: jm@south.america.org
230 Guest login ok, access restrictions apply.
ftp>
```

The password itself will not echo. This is to protect a user's security when he or she is using a real account to FTP files between machines. Once you reach the 'ftp>' prompt, you know you're logged in and ready to go.

Be careful when you answer the Password: prompt! Do not, under any circumstances, use your real system password when using anonymous FTP. There is no reason for a remote system to need your local password. Only give your email address, unless the remote system requires you to type a generic password like 'guest'.

dir: Directory of Files

At the 'ftp>' prompt, you can type a number of commands to perform various functions. One example is 'dir'—it will list the files in the current directory. Continuing the example from above:

```
ftp> dir

200 PORT command successful.
150 Opening ASCII mode data connection for /bin/ls.
total 3116
drwxr-xr-x 2 7   21          512 Nov 21 1988    .forward
-rw-rw-r-- 1 7   11            0 Jun 23 1988    .hushlogin
drwxrwxr-x 2 0   21          512 Jun 4 1990     Census
drwxrwxr-x 2 0   120         512 Jan 8 09:36    ClariNet
            . . . etc etc . . .
-rw-rw-r-- 1 7   14        42390 May 20 02:24   newthisweek.Z
            . . . etc etc . . .
-rw-rw-r-- 1 7   14      2018887 May 21 01:01   uumap.tar.Z
drwxrwxr-x 2 7   6         1024 May 11 10:58    uunet-info

226 Transfer complete.
5414 bytes received in 1.1 seconds (4.9 Kbytes/s)
ftp>
```

The file 'newthisweek.Z' was specifically included because we'll be using it later. Just for general information, it used to be a listing of all the files added to UUNET's archives during a given one-week period.

The directory shown is on a machine running the Unix operating system; the dir command will produce different results on other operating systems (like TOPS, VMS, et al.). Learning to recognize different formats will take some time. After a few weeks of traversing the Internet, it proves easier to see, for example, how large a file is on an operating system you're otherwise not acquainted with.

With many FTP implementations, it's also possible to take the output of dir and put it into a file on the local system with

ftp> dir n* *outfilename*

the contents of which can then be read outside of the live FTP connection; this is particularly useful for systems with very long directories (like ftp.uu.net). The above example would put the names of every file that begins with an 'n' into the local file *outfilename*.

cd: Changing the Current Directory

At the beginning of an FTP session, the user is in a "top-level" directory. Most things are in directories below it (e.g., '/pub'). To change the current directory, one uses the cd command. To change to the directory 'pub', for example, one would type

ftp> cd pub

which would elicit the response

250 CWD command successful.

meaning that the "Change Working Directory" command ('cd') worked properly. Moving "up" a directory is more system-specific—in Unix, use the command 'cd ..' and in VMS, 'cd (-)'.

Keep in mind that many systems are case-sensitive; the directory or file 'Test' is often different from 'test'. If you get in the practice of doing things in lower case, you'll meet with a high degree of success.

get and put: File Transfer

The actual transfer is performed with the get and put commands. To *get* a file from the remote computer to the local system, the command takes the form:

```
ftp> get filename
```

where *filename* is the file on the remote system. Again using ftp.uu.net as an example, the file 'newthisweek.Z' can be retrieved with

```
ftp> get newthisweek.Z
200 PORT command successful.
150 Opening ASCII mode data connection for newthisweek.Z (42390 bytes).
226 Transfer complete.
local: newthisweek.Z remote: newthisweek.Z
42553 bytes received in 6.9 seconds (6 Kbytes/s)
ftp>
```

The section below on using binary mode instead of ASCII will describe why this particular choice will result in a corrupt and subsequently unusable file.

If, for some reason, you want to save a file under a different name (e.g., your system can only have 14-character filenames, or can only have one dot in the name), you can specify what the local filename should be by providing get with an additional argument

```
ftp> get newthisweek.Z uunet-new
```

which will place the contents of the file 'newthisweek.Z' in 'uunet-new' on the local system. This is handy for systems like VMS and MS-DOS, which have restrictions on what a filename can look like. For VMS, if you try to get a file with more than one period in it (e.g., 'foo-1.2.bck'), you will receive an error about an incorrect filename. To avoid this problem, you can use a local filename which only has one period in it:

```
ftp> get foo-1.2.bck foo-1—2.bck
```

Transfers work the other way, too. The put command will transfer a file from the local system to the remote system. If the permissions are set up for an FTP session to write to a remote directory, a file can be sent with

```
ftp> put filename
```

As with get, put will take a second argument, letting you specify a different name for the file on the remote system.

ASCII vs. Binary

In the previous example, the file 'newthisweek.Z' was transferred, but supposedly not correctly. The reason is this: in a normal ASCII transfer (the default), certain characters are translated between systems to help make text files more readable. However, when *binary* files—those containing non-ASCII characters—are transferred, this translation should *not* take place. One example is a binary program: a few changed characters can render it completely useless.

To avoid this problem, it's possible to be in one of two modes—*ASCII* or *binary*. In binary mode, the file isn't translated in any way. What's on the remote system is precisely what's received. The commands to go between the two modes are:

```
ftp> ascii
200 Type set to A. (Note the A, which signifies ASCII mode.)
```

```
ftp> binary
200 Type set to I. (Set to Image format, for pure binary transfers.)
```

Note that each command need only be done once to take effect; if the user types binary, all transfers in that session are done in binary mode (that is, unless ascii is typed later).

The transfer of 'newthisweek.Z' will work if done as:

```
ftp> binary
200 Type set to I.
ftp> get newthisweek.Z
200 PORT command successful.
```

```
150 Opening BINARY mode data connection for newthisweek.Z (42390 bytes).
226 Transfer complete.
local: newthisweek.Z remote: newthisweek.Z
42390 bytes received in 7.2 seconds (5.8 Kbytes/s)
```

Note: The file size (42390) is different from that done in ASCII mode (42553 bytes); and the number 42390 matches the one in the listing of UUNET's top directory. We can be relatively sure that we've received the file without any problems.

mget and mput: Multiple Files

The commands mget and mput allow for multiple file transfers using wildcards to get several files, or a whole set of files at once, rather than having to do it manually, one by one. For example, to get all files that begin with the letter 'f', one would type

```
ftp> mget f*
```

Similarly, to put all of the local files that end with .c:

```
ftp> mput *.c
```

Rather than reiterate what's been written a hundred times before, consult a local manual for more information on wildcard matching (every DOS manual, for example, has a section on it).

Normally, FTP assumes that a user wants to be prompted for every file in an mget or mput operation. You'll often need to get a whole set of files and not have each of them confirmed—you know they're all right. In that case, use the prompt command to turn the queries off.

```
ftp> prompt
Interactive mode off.
```

Likewise, to turn it back on, the prompt command should simply be issued again.

Those '.Z' Files

A large number of the FTP sites around the world are running the Unix operating system. To conserve space, files are often "compressed" down to a smaller, more compact size. The Unix utility (called compress) that performs this operation gives the new file a '.Z' extension. To restore the file to its original size (so you can use it), the uncompress command will work on a Unix system. If you're on a system running VMS, use the public domain program called LZDCM; versions of uncompress have also been ported to MSDOS. For other operating systems, contact your local system administrator or support staff for assistance.

The *archie* Server

A group of people at McGill University in Canada got together and created a query system called *archie*. It was originally formed to be a quick and easy way to scan the offerings of the many anonymous FTP sites that are maintained around the world. As time progressed, archie grew to include other valuable services as well. Its inventors formed a company (see page 89) to meet the rising demand for faster and more stable archie servers and professional support.

The archie databases are accessible through an interactive telnet session, email queries, and command-line and X-window clients. The email responses can be used along with FTPmail servers for those not on the Internet. (See Appendix B, *Retrieving Files via Email,* for information on using FTPmail servers.)

Using archie Today

Currently, archie tracks the contents of over 1000 anonymous FTP archive sites containing over a million files stored across the Internet. Collectively, these files represent well over 50 gigabytes of information, with new entries being added daily.

The archie server automatically updates the listing information from each site about once a month. This avoids constantly updating the databases, which could waste network resources, yet ensures that the information on each site's holdings is reasonably up to date.

To access archie interactively, telnet to one of the many servers around the world[1].

Australia	archie.au
Austria	archie.univie.ac.at
	archie.edvz.uni-linz.ac.at
Canada	archie.uqam.ca
Finland	archie.funet.fi
Germany	archie.th-darmstadt.de
Israel	archie.ac.il
Italy	archie.unipi.it
Japan	archie.wide.ad.jp
	archie.kuis.kyoto-u.ac.jp
Korea	archie.kr
	archie.sogang.ac.kr
New Zealand	archie.nz
Spain	archie.rediris.es
Sweden	archie.luth.se
Switzerland	archie.switch.ch

1. See Chapter 5, *Telnet* for notes on using the telnet program.

Taiwan	archie.ncu.edu.tw
United Kingdom	archie.doc.ic.ac.uk
USA *(Maryland)*	archie.cura.net
(Nebraska)	archie.unl.edu
(New York)	archie.ans.net
(New York, the InterNIC)	archie.internic.net
(New Jersey)	archie.rutgers.edu

At the login: prompt of one of the servers, enter 'archie'—it won't ask for a password. A greeting will be displayed, detailing information about ongoing work in the archie project; the user will be left at an 'archie>' prompt, at which he may enter commands. Using 'help' will yield instructions on using the 'prog' command to make queries, 'set' to control various aspects of the session, and others. Typing 'quit' at the prompt will leave archie. The query 'prog vine.tar.Z' will yield a list of the systems that offer the source to the X-windows program vine; a piece of the information returned looks like:

```
Host ftp.uu.net  (137.39.1.9)
Last updated 10:30 7 Jan 1992

    Location: /packages/X/contrib
      FILE   rw-r--r--   15548 Oct 8 20:29  vine.tar.Z

Host nic.funet.fi  (128.214.6.100)
Last updated 05:07 4 Jan 1992

    Location: /pub/X11/contrib
      FILE   rw-rw-r--   15548 Nov 8 03:25  vine.tar.Z
```

archie *Clients*

There are two mainstream archie clients, one called (naturally enough) 'archie', the other 'xarchie' (for X-Windows). They query the archie databases and yield a list of systems that have the requested file(s) available for anonymous FTP without requiring an interactive session to the server. For example, to find the same information you tried with the server command 'prog', you could type

```
% archie vine.tar.Z
Host athene.uni-paderborn.de
    Location: /local/X11/more—contrib
        FILE -rw-r--r--  18854 Nov 15 1990 vine.tar.Z

Host emx.cc.utexas.edu
    Location: /pub/mnt/source/games
        FILE -rw-r--r--  12019 May 7 1988 vine.tar.Z

Host export.lcs.mit.edu
    Location: /contrib
        FILE -rw-r--r--  15548 Oct 9 00:29 vine.tar.Z
```

Note that your system administrator may not have installed the archie clients yet; the source is available on each of the archie servers, in the directory 'archie/clients'.

Using the X-windows client is much more intuitive—if it's installed, just read its man page and give it a whirl. It's essential for the networked desktop.

Mailing archie

Users limited to email connectivity to the Internet should send a message to the address 'archie@archie.sura.net' with the single word help in the body of the message. An email message will be returned, explaining how to use the email archie server—most of the commands offered by the telnet interface are available.

The same rules hold with email requests as with use of the telnet interface. If you pick an archie server that's close to you, the turn-around time for a query will be very short.

The whatis Database

In addition to offering access to anonymous FTP listings, archie also provides access to the *whatis* description database. It includes the names and brief synopses of thousands of public domain software packages, datasets, and informational documents located on the Internet.

To search the database, simply log into an Archie server and issue the command 'whatis'. For example, to find packages that offer calendar programs and such, one would use

```
archie> whatis calendar

cal                 Print calendar
cal-entries         Long list of entries for input to calendar(1)
calen               Calendar program
calend-remind       A souped-up implementation of the UNIX calendar(1)
calendar            Calendar program
calgen              Calendar generation program
do                  A calendar-like utility
month               Visual calendar program
monthtool           Monthly appointment calendar, for Suns
pcal                Calendar program, 1 month per page
perpetual           The Last Perpetual Calendar
xcal                A calendar program (X11)
xcalendar           A personal schedule maintainer in X11
xdiary              X11 based calendar and diary
xkal                X11 appointment calendar
```

Additional *whatis* databases are scheduled to be added in the future. Planned offerings include listings for the names and locations of online library catalog programs, the names of publicly accessible electronic mailing lists, compilations of Frequently Asked Questions lists, and archive sites for the most popular Usenet newsgroups. Suggestions for additional descriptions or locations are welcomed, and should be sent to the archie developers at 'archie-group@bunyip.com'.

"Was für ein Platz zum plünder!"
("What a place to plunder!")

— Gebhard Leberecht Blücher

4 Usenet News

The first thing to understand about Usenet is that it is widely misunderstood. Every day on Usenet the "blind men and the elephant" phenomenon appears, in spades. In the opinion of the author, more *flame wars* (rabid arguments) arise because of a lack of understanding of the nature of Usenet than from any other source. And consider that such flame wars arise, of necessity, among people who are on Usenet. Imagine, then, how poorly understood Usenet must be by those outside!

No essay on the nature of Usenet can ignore the erroneous impressions held by many Usenet users. Therefore, this section will also treat the falsehoods. Keep reading for truth. (Beauty, alas, is not relevant to Usenet.)

What Usenet Is

Usenet is the set of machines that exchange articles tagged with one or more universally recognized labels, called *newsgroups* (or "groups" for short). (Note that the term "newsgroup" is correct, while "area," "base," "board," "bboard," "conference," "round table," "SIG," etc., are all incorrect. If you want to be understood, be accurate.)

The Diversity of Usenet

If the above definition of Usenet sounds vague, that's because it is. It's almost impossible to generalize over all Usenet sites in any nontrivial way. Usenet encompasses government agencies, large universities, high schools, businesses of all sizes, home computers of all descriptions, etc.

Every administrator controls that person's own site. No one has any real control over any site but his or her own. The administrator gets that power from the owner of the system being administrated. As long as the owner is happy with the job the administrator is doing, the administrator can do whatever he or she pleases, up to and including cutting off Usenet entirely. *C'est la vie.*

What Usenet Is Not

➡️ *Usenet is not an organization.*

Usenet has no central authority. In fact, it has no central anything. There is a vague notion of "upstream" and "downstream" related to the direction of high-volume news flow. It follows that, the extent "upstream" sites decide what traffic they will carry for their "downstream" neighbors, "upstream" sites have some influence on their neighbors. However, such influence is usually easy to circumvent, and heavy-handed manipulation typically results in a backlash of resentment.

➡️ *Usenet is not a democracy.*

A democracy can be loosely defined as "government of the people, by the people, for the people." However, as explained above, Usenet is not an organization, and only an organization can be run as a democracy. Even a democracy must be organized, for if it lacks a means of enforcing the people's wishes, it may as well not exist.

Some people wish that Usenet were a democracy. Many people pretend that it is. Both groups are sadly deluded.

➡️ *Usenet is not fair.*

After all, who decides what's fair? For that matter, if someone behaves unfairly, who's going to stop him? Neither you nor I, that's certain.

➡️ *Usenet is not a right.*

Some people misunderstand their local right of "freedom of speech" to mean that they have a legal right to use others' computers to say what they wish in whatever way they wish, and the owners of said computers have no right to stop them.

Those people are wrong. Freedom of speech also means freedom not to speak; if I choose not to use my computer to aid your speech, that is my right. Freedom of the press belongs to those who own one.

➡ *Usenet is not a public utility.*

Some Usenet sites are publicly funded or subsidized. Most of them, by plain count, are not. There is no government monopoly on Usenet, and little or no control.

➡ *Usenet is not a commercial network.*

Many Usenet sites are academic or government organizations; in fact, Usenet originated in academia. Therefore, there is a Usenet custom of keeping commercial traffic to a minimum. If such commercial traffic is generally considered worth carrying, then it may, grudgingly, be tolerated. Even so, it is usually separated somehow from noncommercial traffic—for example, in the newsgroup comp.newprod and the hierarchy biz.

➡ *Usenet is not the Internet.*

The Internet is a wide-ranging network, parts of which are subsidized by various governments. The Internet carries many kinds of traffic; Usenet is only one of them. So, the Internet is only one of the various networks carrying Usenet traffic.

➡ *Usenet is not a Unix network, nor even an ASCII network.*

Don't assume that everyone is using rn on a Unix machine. There are VAXen running VMS, IBM mainframes, Amigas, and MS-DOS PCs reading and posting to Usenet. And yes, some of them use (shudder) EBCDIC. Ignore them if you like, but they're out there.

➡ *Usenet is not software.*

There are dozens of software packages used at various sites to transport and read Usenet articles. Thus, no one program or package can be called "the Usenet software."

Software designed to support Usenet traffic can be (and is) used for other kinds of communication, usually without risk of mixing the two. Such private communication networks are typically kept distinct from Usenet by the invention of newsgroup names different from the universally recognized ones.

➡ *Usenet is not a UUCP network.*

UUCP is a protocol (some might say *protocol suite*, but that's a technical point) for sending data over point-to-point connections, typically using dial-up modems. Usenet is only one of the various kinds of traffic carried via UUCP, and UUCP is only one of the various transports carrying Usenet traffic.

Well, enough negativity.

Propagation of News

In the old days, when UUCP over long-distance dial-up lines was the dominant means of article transmission, a few well-connected sites had real influence in determining which newsgroups would be carried where. Those sites called themselves "the backbone."

But things have changed. Nowadays, even the smallest Internet site has connectivity the likes of which the backbone admin of yesteryear could only dream. In addition, in the U.S., the advent of cheaper long-distance calls and high-speed modems has made long-distance Usenet feeds thinkable for smaller companies. UUNET is the only preeminent UUCP transport site today in the U.S. It isn't a player in the propagation wars, though, because it never refuses any traffic—it gets paid by the minute, after all; to refuse based on content would jeopardize its legal status as an enhanced service provider.

All of the above applies to the U.S. In Europe, different cost structures favored the creation of strictly controlled hierarchical organizations with central registries. This is all very unlike the traditional mode of U.S. sites (pick a name, get the software, get a feed, you're on). Europe's "benign monopolies," long uncontested, now face competition from looser organizations patterned after the U.S. model.

Reading News

 How you actually access Usenet newsgroups varies dramatically from one system to another. On Unix systems alone, there are at least seven different news readers you can use. Your best bet is to ask your support staff or system administrator how to read news on your local system. Under Unix, rn, trn, and nn are common news readers. With VMS, the command is often NEWS.

Common to all news readers is a list of groups that you want to read. This list can be very large (in excess of 2,000 groups in many cases); don't start to blink in wonder and question why you even bothered trying. Most of these files have a sensible format to them, and you can "unsubscribe" to everything at once, and then only subscribe to the things you're really interested in. For example, most Unix newsreaders use a '.newsrc' file, which lists each group with either a colon (you're subscribed) or an exclamation point (you're not) after the name. Using your favorite text editor, you should be able to replace all of the colons with exclamation points, and then start trolling down the list, picking things you think you might be interested in.

Group Creation

 As discussed above, Usenet is not a democracy. Nevertheless, currently the most popular way to create a new newsgroup involves a "vote" to determine popular support for (and opposition to) a proposed newsgroup. See Appendix C, *Newsgroup Creation*, for detailed instructions on and guidelines for the process involved in making a newsgroup.

If you follow the guidelines, it is probable that your group will be created and widely propagated. However, due to the nature of Usenet, there is no way for any user to enforce the results of a newsgroup vote (or any other decision, for that matter). Therefore, for your new newsgroup to be propagated widely, you must not only follow the letter of the guidelines; you must also follow their spirit. And you must not allow even a whiff of shady dealings or dirty tricks to mar the vote.

So, you may ask: How is a new user supposed to know anything about the "spirit" of the guidelines? Obviously, he can't. This fact leads inexorably to the following recommendation:

If you're a new user, don't try to create a new newsgroup alone.

If you have a good newsgroup idea, read the news.groups newsgroup for a while (six months, at least) to find out how things work. If you're too impatient to wait six months, you really need to learn; read news.groups for a year instead. If you just can't wait, find an old Usenet hand to run the vote for you.

Readers may think this advice unnecessarily strict. Ignore it at your peril. It is embarrassing to speak before learning. It is foolish to jump into a society you don't understand with your mouth open. And it is futile to try to force your will on people who can tune you out with the press of a key.

Bogus Newsgroups

Occasionally, people will take advantage of the Usenet newsgroup mechanism and create "fake" newsgroups. They have included names like alt.swedish-chef.bork.bork.bork, etc. While they can occasionally be funny, they cause no small amount of grief for news administrators. If you do figure out how to fake a control message to create a group, just pride yourself on your ingenuity—you and everyone else will be much happier.

If You're Unhappy. . .

Property rights being what they are, there is no higher authority on Usenet than the people who own the machines on which Usenet traffic is carried. If the owner of the machine you use says, "We will not carry alt.sex on this machine,"

and you are not happy with that order, you have no Usenet recourse. What can we outsiders do, after all?

That doesn't mean you are without options. Depending on the nature of your site, you may have some internal political recourse. Or you might find external pressure helpful. Or, with a minimal investment, you can get a feed of your own from somewhere else. The everyday personal computer is capable of receiving a Usenet feed now, Unix-capable boxes are going for under $2000, and there are at least two Unix looka-likes in the $100 price range.

No matter what, appealing to the Net won't help. Even if those who read such an appeal regarding system administration are sympathetic to your cause, they will almost certainly have even less influence at your site than you do.

By the same token, if you don't like what some user at another site is doing, only the administrator and/or owner of that site have any authority to do anything about it. Persuade them that the user in question is a problem for them, and they might do something (if they feel like it). If the user in question is the administrator or owner of the site from which he or she posts, forget it; you can't win. Arrange for your newsreading software to ignore articles from him or her if you can, and chalk one up to experience.

The History of Usenet (The ABCs)

 In the beginning, there were conversations, and they were good. Then came Usenet in 1979, shortly after the release of V7 Unix with UUCP; and it was better. Two Duke University grad students in North Carolina, Tom Truscott and Jim Ellis, thought of hooking computers together to exchange information with the Unix community. Steve Bellovin, a grad student at the University of North Carolina, put together the first version of the news software using shell scripts and installed it on the first two sites: *unc* and *duke.* At the beginning of 1980, the network consisted of those two sites and *phs* (another machine at Duke), and was described at the January

1980 Usenix conference in Boulder, CO.[1] Steve Bellovin later rewrote the scripts into C programs, but they were never released beyond *unc* and *duke*. Shortly thereafter, Steve Daniel did another implementation in the C programming language for public distribution. Tom Truscott made further modifications, and this became the "A" news release.

In 1981 at the University of California at Berkeley, grad student Mark Horton and high school student Matt Glickman rewrote the news software to add functionality and to cope with the ever increasing volume of news—"A" news was intended for only a few articles per group per day. This rewrite was the "B" news version. The first public release was version 2.1 in 1982; all versions before 2.1 were considered in beta test. As the Net grew, the news software was expanded and modified. The last version maintained and released primarily by Mark was 2.10.1.

Rick Adams, then at the Center for Seismic Studies, took over coordination of the maintenance and enhancement of the news software with the 2.10.2 release in 1984. By this time, the increasing volume of news was becoming a concern, and the mechanism for moderated groups was added to the software at 2.10.2. Moderated groups were inspired by ARPA mailing lists and experience with other bulletin board systems. In late 1986, version 2.11 of news was released, including a number of changes to support a new naming structure for newsgroups, enhanced batching and compression, enhanced ihave/sendme control messages, and other features. The current release of news is 2.11, patchlevel 19.

A new version of news, known as "C" news, was developed at the University of Toronto by Geoff Collyer and Henry Spencer. This version is a rewrite of the lowest levels of news to increase article processing speed, decrease article expiration processing, and improve the reliability of the news system through better locking, etc. The package was released to the Net in the Autumn of 1987. For more information, see the paper *News Need Not Be Slow*, published in the Winter 1987 Usenix Technical Conference proceedings.

1. The Usenix conferences are semi-annual meetings at which members of the Usenix Association, a group of Unix enthusiasts, meet and trade notes.

Usenet software has also been ported to a number of platforms, from the Amiga and IBM PCs all the way to minicomputers and mainframes.

Hierarchies

Newsgroups are organized according to their specific areas of concentration. Since the groups are in a *tree* structure, the various areas are called hierarchies. There are seven major categories:

comp	Topics of interest to both computer professionals and hobbyists, including topics in computer science, software sources, and information on hardware and software systems.
misc	Groups that are neither fish, flesh, nor fowl usually end up being part of the misc hierarchy. Subjects include fitness, job-hunting, law, and investments.
sci	Discussions marked by special knowledge relating to research in or application of the established sciences.
soc	Groups primarily addressing social issues and socializing. Included are discussions related to many different world cultures.
talk	Groups largely debate-oriented and tending to feature long discussions without resolution and without appreciable amounts of generally useful information.
news	Groups concerned with the news network, group maintenance, and software.
rec	Groups oriented toward hobbies and recreational activities.

These "world" newsgroups are (usually) circulated around the entire Usenet—this implies worldwide distribution. Not all groups actually enjoy such wide distribution, however. The European Usenet and Eunet sites take only a selected subset of the more "technical" groups, and controversial "noise" groups are often not carried by many sites in the U.S. and Canada (these groups are primarily under the 'talk' and 'soc' classifications). Many sites do not carry some or all of the comp.binaries groups because of the typically large size of the posts in them (being actual executable programs).

Also available are a number of "alternative" hierarchies:

alt	True anarchy; anything and everything can and does appear; subjects include sex, the Simpsons, and privacy.
gnu	Groups concentrating on interests and software with the GNU Project of the Free Software Foundation (see page 101).
biz	Business-related groups.

Moderated vs. Unmoderated

Some newsgroups insist that the discussion remain focused and on target; to serve this need, moderated groups were invented. All articles posted to a moderated group get mailed to the group's *moderator*. He or she periodically (hopefully sooner than later) reviews the posts, and then either posts them individually to Usenet, or posts a composite *digest* of the articles for the past day or two. This is how many mailing list gateways work (e.g., the *Risks Digest*).

news.groups and news.announce.newgroups

Being a good *net.citizen* includes being involved in the continuing growth and evolution of the Usenet system. One part of this involvement includes following the discussion in the groups news.groups and the notes in news.announce.–

`newgroups`. It is there that discussion goes on about the creation of new groups and the destruction of inactive ones. Every person on Usenet is allowed and encouraged to vote on the creation of a newsgroup.

Weekly, the moderator of `news.announce.newgroups` posts updates detailing the votes that are running, those that have passed, and other information. By reading these, you can stay informed and do not need to wade through the usually high-traffic `news.groups`.

How Usenet Works

The transmission of Usenet news is entirely cooperative. Feeds are generally provided out of good will and the desire to distribute news everywhere. There are places that provide feeds for a fee (e.g., UUNET), but for the large part no exchange of money is involved.

There are two major transport methods, UUCP and NNTP. The first is mainly modem-based and involves the normal charges for telephone calls. The second, NNTP, is the primary method for distributing news over the Internet.

With UUCP, news is stored in *batches* on a site until the neighbor calls to receive the articles, or the feed site happens to call. A list of groups that the neighbor wishes to receive is maintained on the feed site. The Cnews system compresses its batches, which can dramatically reduce the transmission time necessary for a relatively heavy newsfeed.

NNTP, on the other hand, offers a little more latitude with how news is sent. The traditional store-and-forward method is, of course, available. Given the "real-time" nature of the Internet, though, other methods have been devised. Programs now keep constant connections with their news neighbors, sending news nearly instantaneously, and can handle dozens of simultaneous feeds, both incoming and outgoing.

The transmission of a Usenet article is centered around the unique 'Message-ID:' header. When an NNTP site offers an article to a neighbor, it says it has that specific Message ID. If the neighbor finds it hasn't received the article yet, it tells the feed to send it through; this is repeated for each and every article that's waiting for the neighbor. Using unique

IDs helps prevent a system from receiving five copies of an article from each of its five news neighbors, for example.

Further information on how Usenet works with relation to the various transports is available in the documentation for the Cnews and NNTP packages, as well as in RFC-1036, the *Standard for Interchange of USENET Messages,* and RFC-977, *Network News Transfer Protocol: A Proposed Standard for the Stream-Based Transmission of News.* The RFCs do tend to be rather dry reading, particularly to the new user. (See page 122, for information on retrieving RFCs.)

Mail Gateways

A natural progression is for Usenet news and electronic mailing lists to somehow become merged—which they have, in the form of *news gateways.* Many mailing lists are set up to "reflect" messages not only to the readership of the list, but also into a newsgroup. Likewise, posts to a newsgroup can be sent to the moderator of the mailing list, or to the entire mailing list. Some examples of this in action are `comp.risks` (the *Risks Digest*) and `comp.dcom.telecom` (the *Telecom Digest*).

This method of propagating mailing-list traffic has helped solve the problem of a single message being delivered to a number of people at the same site—instead, anyone can just subscribe to the group. Also, mailing-list maintenance is lowered substantially, since the moderators don't have to be constantly removing and adding users to and from the list. Instead, the people can read and not read the newsgroup at their leisure.

Usenet "Netiquette"

There are many traditions with Usenet, not the least of which is dubbed *netiquette*—being polite and considerate of others. If you follow a few basic guidelines, you, and everyone that reads your posts, will be much happier in the long run.

Signatures

At the end of most articles is a small blurb called a person's *signature*, or just "sig". In Unix this file is named '.signature' in the person's login directory—it will vary for other operating systems. It exists to provide information about how to get in touch with the person posting the article, including their email address, phone number, address, or where they're located. Even so, signatures have become the graffiti of computers. People put song lyrics, pictures, philosophical quotes, and even advertisements in their ".sigs". (Note, however, that advertising in your signature will more often than not get you *flamed* until you take it out.)

Four lines will suffice—more is just extra garbage for Usenet sites to carry along with your article, which is supposed to be the intended focus of the reader. Netiquette dictates limiting oneself to this "quota" of four—some people make signatures that are ten lines or even more, including elaborate ASCII drawings of their hand-written signature or faces or even the space shuttle. This is not cute, and will bother people to no end.

The newsgroup alt.fan.warlord is a dumping ground for the most heinous of signature violations. In the course of reading news, people occasionally do follow-ups into alt.fan.warlord to show off their latest discoveries—talking whales, ten-line-high cacti, and a variety of other ASCII miracles.

It's also not absolutely necessary to include a signature—if you forget to append it to an article, *don't worry about it.* The article's just as good as it ever would be, and contains everything you should want to say. Don't re-post the article just to make sure people see your sig.

Posting Personal Messages

If mail to a person doesn't make it through, avoid posting the message to a newsgroup. Even if the likelihood of that person reading the group is very high, all of the other people reading the articles don't give a whit what you have to say to Jim Morrison. Simply wait for the person to post again and double-check the address, or get in touch with your system administrator and see if it's a problem with local email delivery. It may also turn out that the person's site is down or is having problems, in which case it's just necessary to wait until things return to normal before contacting Jim.

Posting Mail

In the interests of privacy, it's considered extremely bad taste to post any email that someone may have sent, unless they explicitly give you permission to redistribute it. While the legal issues can be heavily debated, most everyone agrees that email should be treated as anything one would receive via normal snailmail,[2] preserving all of the assumed rights it carries.

Test Messages

Many people, particularly new users, want to try out posting before actually taking part in discussions. Often, the mechanics of getting messages out is the most difficult part of Usenet. To this end, many, many users find it necessary to post their tests to "normal" groups (for example, news.admin or comp.mail.misc). This is considered a major netiquette *faux pas* in the Usenet world. There are a number of groups available, called *test groups*, which exist solely for the purpose of trying out a news system, reader, or even new signature. They include:

```
alt.test
gnu.gnusenet.test
misc.test
```

some of which will generate *auto-magic* replies to your posts to let you know they made it through. There are certain denizens of Usenet who frequent the test groups to help new users out. They respond to the posts, often including the article so the poster can see how it got to the person's site. Also, many regional hierarchies have test groups, like phl.test in Philadelphia.

By all means, experiment and test—just do it in its proper place.

2. The slang for the normal land and air postal service.

Famous People Appearing

Every once in a while, someone says that a celebrity is accessible through the Net; or, even more entertaining, an article is forged to appear to be coming from that celebrity. One example of this is with Stephen Spielberg— the rec.arts.movies readership was in an uproar for two weeks following a couple of posts supposedly made by Mr. Spielberg. (Some detective work revealed it to be a hoax.)

There are a few well-known people who are acquainted with Usenet and networks in general—but the overwhelming majority are just normal people. One should act with skepticism whenever a notable personality is "seen" in a newsgroup.

Summaries

Authors of articles occasionally say that readers should reply by mail and they'll *summarize*. Accordingly, readers should do just that—reply via mail. Responding with a follow-up article to such an article defeats the intention of the author. In a few days, he will post one article containing the highlights of the responses he received. By following up to the whole group, the author may not read what you have to say.

When creating a summary of the replies to a post, try to make it as *reader-friendly* as possible. Avoid just putting all of the messages received into one big file. Rather, take some time and edit the messages into a form that contains only the essential information that other readers would be interested in.

Sometimes people will respond but request to remain anonymous (one example might be employees who feel the information's not proprietary, but at the same time want to protect themselves from political backlash in their company). Summaries should honor this request accordingly by listing the 'From:' address as 'anonymous' or '(Address withheld by request).'

Quoting

When following up to an article, many newsreaders provide the facility to *quote* the original article with each line prefixed by '>', as in

```
In article <1232@foo.bar.com>, sharon@foo.bar.com wrote:
> I agree, I think that basketweaving's really catching on,
> particularly in Pennsylvania. Here's a list of every person
> in PA that currently engages in it publicly:
            . . . etc . . .
```

This is a severe example (potentially a horribly long article), but proves a point. When you quote another person, *edit out* whatever isn't directly applicable to your reply.[3] This gives the reader of the new article a better idea of the points you were addressing. By including the *entire* article, you'll only annoy those reading it. Also, signatures in the original aren't necessary; the readers already know who wrote it (by the attribution).

Avoid being tedious with responses—rather than pick apart an article, address it in parts or as a whole. Addressing practically each and every word in an article only proves that the person responding has absolutely nothing better to do with his time.

If a "war" starts (insults and personal comments get thrown back and forth), *take it into email*—exchange email with the person you're arguing with. No one enjoys watching people bicker incessantly.

Crossposting

The 'Newsgroups:' line isn't limited to just one group—an article can be posted in a list of groups. For instance, the line

```
Newsgroups: sci.space,comp.simulation
```

posts the article to both the groups sci.space and comp.simulation. It's usually safe to crosspost to up to three or four groups. To list more than that is considered "excessive noise."

3. But not changing their words along the way, of course.

It's also suggested that if an article is crossposted, a 'Followup-To:' header should be included. It should name the group to which all additional discussion should be directed. For the above example, a possible 'Followup-To:' would be

    Followup-To: sci.space

which would make all follow-ups automatically posted to just sci.space, rather than to both sci.space and comp.simulation. If every response made with a newsreader's "followup" command should go to the person posting the article no matter what, there's also a mechanism worked in to accommodate this. The 'Followup-To:' header should contain the single word "poster":

    Followup-To: poster

Certain newsreaders will use this to sense that a reply should never be posted back onto the Net. This is often used with questions that will yield a summary of information later, a vote, or an advertisement.

A Dying Boy's Last Wish

At least once every two to three months someone re-posts a request from a dying boy whose only desire is to get into the *Guinness Book of World Records* as having received the most postcards in history.

Over 33 million postcards were received by May 1991, and they continued to pour in. Craig achieved his goal, and was in the 1992 U.S. edition (see page 207); Guinness was so bothered by the volume of the response from the world community that they have discontinued the category. Craig is also fine—he was flown to Las Vegas by a generous businessman and treated by specialists.

As the Usenet Frequently Asked Questions list suggests, send the cost of postage to a worthy cause like UNICEF or the International Red Cross instead. There are many, many dying children who are just as needful of your support as Craig was.

Recent News

One should avoid posting "recent" events—sports scores, a plane crash, or whatever people will see on the evening news or read in the morning paper. By the time the article has propagated across all of Usenet, the "news" value of the article will have become stale. (This is one case for the argument that "Usenet news" is a misnomer.[4])

Computer Religion

No matter what kind of computer a person is using, it is always the *best* and most efficient of them all. Posting articles asking questions like 'What computer should I buy? An Atari ST or an Amiga?' will lead only to fervent arguments over the merits and drawbacks of each brand. Don't even ask the Net—go to a local user group, or do some research of your own like reading some magazine reviews. Trying to say that one computer is somehow better than another is a moot point.

If you really need to make a point, Bill Wisner of the University of Alaska started a group called alt.religion.computers; in it, you may feel free to expound upon the virtues of your favorite computer manufacturer, operating system, or any other facet you deem worthy.

Quality of Postings

How you write and present yourself in your articles is important. If you have terrible spelling, keep a dictionary nearby. If you have trouble with grammar and punctuation, try to get a book on English grammar and composition (found in many bookstores and at garage sales). By all means pay attention to what you say—it makes you who you are on the Net.

Likewise, try to be clear in what you ask. Ambiguous or vague questions often lead to no response at all, leaving the poster discouraged. Give as much essential information as you feel is necessary to let people help you, but keep it within limits. For instance, you should probably include the operating system of your computer in

---

4. Note that the ClariNet News service (see page 89) offers news items in a Usenet format as a precise *alternative* to the morning paper.

the post if it's needed, but don't tell everybody what peripherals you have hanging off of it.

Useful Subjects

The 'Subject:' line of an article is what will first attract people to read it—if it's vague or doesn't describe what's contained within, no one will read the article. At the same time, 'Subject:' lines that are too wordy tend to be irritating. For example:

Subject: Building Emacs on a Sun Sparc under 4.1

Subject: Tryin' to find Waldo in NJ.

Subject: I can't get emacs to work!!!

Subject: I'm desperately in search of the honorable Mr. Waldo in the state of. . .

Simply put, try to think of what will best help the reader when he or she encounters your article in a newsreading session.

Tone of Voice

Since common computers can't portray the inflection or tone in a person's voice, how articles are worded can directly affect the response to them. Suppose a discussion about older computing technology were going on; if you posted an article containing the remark

Anybody using a Vic-20 should go buy themselves a life.

you'd definitely get some responses—telling you to take a leap. Rather than being inflammatory, phrase your articles in a way that rationally expresses your opinion, like

What're the practical uses of a Vic-20 these days?

which presents yourself as a much more level-headed individual.

Also, what case (upper or lower) you use can indicate how you're trying to speak—netiquette dictates that if you USE ALL CAPITAL LET-

TERS, people will think you're "shouting." Write as you would in a normal letter to a friend, following traditional rules of English (or whatever language you happen to speak).

Frequently Asked Questions

A number of groups have a *Frequently Asked Questions* (FAQ) list, which gives the answers to questions or points that have been raised time and time again. FAQs are intended to help cut down redundant traffic. For example, in alt.tv.simpsons, one recurring question is, "Did you notice that there's a different blackboard opening at the beginning of every Simpsons episode?" As a result, it's part of the FAQ for that group.

Usually, FAQ lists are posted at the beginning of each month and set to expire one month later (when, supposedly, the next FAQ will be published). Nearly every FAQ is also crossposted to news.answers, which is used as a Usenet repository for them.

The RTFM Archive

In 1991, Jonathan Kamens, then of MIT, graciously set up a machine dedicated to the archiving and storage of the many periodic postings that are peppered throughout the various Usenet groups. Since he left, the staff at MIT has continued to maintain this service. To access the archive, FTP to the system rtfm.mit.edu and look in the directory '/pub/usenet'.

"Be it true or false, so it be news."

— Ben Jonson, *News from the New World*

A Final Note

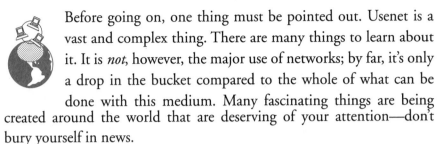

Before going on, one thing must be pointed out. Usenet is a vast and complex thing. There are many things to learn about it. It is *not*, however, the major use of networks; by far, it's only a drop in the bucket compared to the whole of what can be done with this medium. Many fascinating things are being created around the world that are deserving of your attention—don't bury yourself in news.

5 Telnet

T*elnet* is the main Internet protocol for creating an interactive connection with a remote machine. It gives the user the opportunity to be on one computer system and do work on another, which may be across the street or thousands of miles away. Distance no longer dictates the costs involved in creating connections—your organization (or you personally) most likely pay a set monthly fee for connectivity, regardless of what systems you communicate with. The ability to work with colleagues from around the world, explore the Net, and travel throughout Cyberspace, all from the comfort of your own office, home, or school, offers an unparalleled opportunity for discovery.

Using Telnet

As with FTP (see Chapter 3, *Anonymous FTP*), the actual command for negotiating a telnet connection varies from system to system. The most common is 'telnet' itself. It takes the form of:

telnet *somewhere.domain*

To be safe, we'll use your local system as a working example. By now, you hopefully know your site's FQDN. If not, *ask* or try to figure it out. You won't get by without it.

To open the connection, type

telnet *your.system.name*

If the system were wubba.cs.widener.edu, for example, the command would look like

```
telnet wubba.cs.widener.edu
```

The system will respond with something similar to

```
Trying 147.31.254.999...
Connected to wubba.cs.widener.edu.
Escape character is '^)'.
```

The escape *character*, in this example '^)' (hold down Control and type a right bracket), is the character that will let you go back to the local system to close the connection, suspend it, etc. To close this connection, the user would type '^)', and respond to the telnet> prompt with the command 'close'. Local documentation should be checked for information on specific commands, functions, and the escape character that can be used.

Telnet Ports

Many telnet clients also include a second option, the *port* on which the connection should take place. Normally, port 23 is the default telnet port; the user never has to think about it. But sometimes it's desirable to telnet to a different port on a system, where there may be a service available, or to aid in debugging a problem. Using

telnet *somewhere.domain port*

will connect the user to the given *port* on the system *somewhere.domain*. Again, this syntax is only approximate (some systems may use telnet *somewhere.domain*/PORT=*port*) and will vary from one operating system to another.

Many libraries use this port method to offer their facilities to the general Internet community; other services are also available. For instance, one would type

```
telnet martini.eecs.umich.edu 3000
```

to connect to the geographic server at the University of Michigan (see page 65). Other such port connections follow the same usage.

Publicly Accessible Libraries

Over the last several years, most university libraries have switched from a manual (card) catalog system to computerized library catalogs. The automated systems provide users with easily accessible and up-to-date information about the books available in these libraries. This has been further improved upon with the advent of local area networks, dial-up modems, and wide area networks (WANs). Now many of us can check on our local library's holdings, or those of a library halfway around the world!

Many, many institutions of higher learning have made their library catalogs available for searching by anyone on the Internet. They include Boston University, the Colorado Alliance of Research Libraries (CARL), and London University King's College.

To include a listing of some of the existing sites would not only be far too long for this document, it would soon be out of date. Instead, several lists are being maintained and are available either by mail or via FTP. Also, the InterNIC *Directory of Directories* also describes the libraries that are accessible (see page 120 for further information).

Art St. George and Ron Larsen are maintaining a list of Internet-accessible libraries and databases often referred to as "the St. George directory." It began with only library catalogs but has expanded to include sections on other resources, from campus-wide information systems to bulletin-board systems that are not on the Internet. The library catalog sections are divided into those that are free, those that charge, and international (i.e., non-U.S.) catalogs; they are arranged by state, province, or country within each section. There is also a section giving dial-up information for some of the library catalogs. It's available for FTP (see Chapter 3, *Anonymous FTP*) on nic.cerf.net in the directory 'cerfnet/cerfnet_info/library_catalog'. The file 'internetcatalogs' has a date suffix; check for the most current date. The information is updated periodically.

Billy Barron, Systems Manager at the University of North Texas, produces a directory as an aid to his user community. It complements the St. George guide by providing a standard format for all systems, listing the Internet address, login instructions, the system vendor, and logoff information. The arrangement is alphabetic by organization name. It's available for FTP on ftp.unt.edu in the directory 'pub/library' as the file 'libraries.txt'.

For announcements of new libraries available and discussion on related topics, consult the Usenet newsgroup comp.internet.library. (See Chapter 4, *Usenet News*, to learn about Usenet.)

Internet Services List

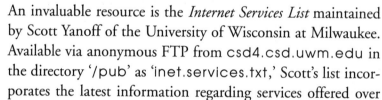

An invaluable resource is the *Internet Services List* maintained by Scott Yanoff of the University of Wisconsin at Milwaukee. Available via anonymous FTP from csd4.csd.uwm.edu in the directory '/pub' as 'inet.services.txt,' Scott's list incorporates the latest information regarding services offered over the Internet. Updates tend to come once every couple of weeks; they are also posted to the Usenet newsgroup alt.bbs.internet. A lot of the work that went into the rest of this chapter is derived from Scott's own achievements.

HYTELNET

Peter Scott of the University of Saskatchewan Library Systems Department created a remarkably useful program called *HYTELNET*; it provides a front end to accessing the Internet's many offerings. Every system mentioned in this chapter, plus many others, are reachable through HYTELNET's easy-to-use screen interface. Librarians have found the program particularly useful for searching library holdings halfway around the world without paying exorbitant communications fees.

Rather than have the user try to remember the procedure for each available system, HYTELNET maintains a database of the necessary details for you, providing the information needed when you decide to explore a given database, library, or other resource. It combines the knowledge of all of the previously mentioned library and service lists into a cohesive and comprehensive system. In early 1992, HYTELNET was awarded the "Research and Education Networking Application Award" by Meckler Publishing.

The directory '/pub/hytelnet' on access.usask.ca houses the source code for the system—contact your system administrator about having it installed on your local system. The program originally supported the IBM PC and compatibles; support for Unix and VMS was added by Earl Fogel.

If you'd like to try out HYTELNET before setting it up locally, telnet to access.usask.ca and log in as 'hytelnet'. To be notified of updates to HYTELNET, you will need to join the 'LIB_HYTELNET' mailing list; contact Peter at 'scott@sklib.usask.ca' to be added. He can be reached conventionally at:

Peter Scott
Systems Department
Univ. of Saskatchewan Libraries
Saskatoon, Saskatchewan, Canada S7N OWO
(306) 966-6014

The Cleveland Freenet

Freenets are open-access, free, community computer systems. One such system is the Cleveland Freenet, sponsored by CWRU (Case Western Reserve University). Anyone and everyone is welcome to join and take part in the exciting project—that of a National Telecomputing Public Network, where everyone benefits. There's *no* charge for the registration process and no charge to use the system.

To register, telnet to any one of

freenet-in-a.cwru.edu

freenet-in-b.cwru.edu
freenet-in-c.cwru.edu

After you're connected, choose the entry on the menu that signifies you're a guest user. Another menu will follow; select 'Apply for an account,' and you'll be well on your way to being a FreeNet member.

You will need to fill out a form and send it to them through the postal service—your login ID and password will be created in a short period of time. At that point you're free to use the system as you wish. They provide multi-user chat, email, Usenet news, and a variety of other things to keep you occupied for hours on end.

Directories

 There are a few systems that are maintained to provide the Internet community with access to lists of information—users, organizations, etc. They range from fully dedicated computers with access to papers and research results to a system to find out about the faculty members of a university.

Knowbot

Knowbot is a "master directory" that contains email address information from the NIC WHOIS database (see page 84), the PSI WhitePages Pilot Project, the NYSERNET X.500 database, and MCI Mail. Most of these services are email registries themselves, but Knowbot provides a very comfortable way to access all of them in one place. Telnet to nri.reston.va.us on port 185.

White Pages

PSI maintains a directory of information on individuals. It will list the person's name, organization, and email address if it is given. Telnet to wp.psi.net and log in as 'fred'. The White Pages Project also includes an interface to use Xwindows remotely.

Databases and Other Resources

 For information on database services, see page 89. Not all databases on the Internet require payment for use, though. There do exist some, largely research-driven, databases that are publicly accessible. New ones spring up regularly.

To find out more about the databases in this section, contact the people directly responsible for them. Their areas of concentration and the software used to implement them are widely disparate. Also, don't forget to check with your local library—the reference librarian there can provide information on conventional resources, and possibly even those available over the Internet (they are becoming more common).

AMS E-Math

The American Mathematical Society (AMS) maintains a system for members of the AMS to learn about professional opportunities and new software. In addition, information on submitting reviews to *Mathematical Reviews* can be obtained by providing the system with your email address, and author lookups can be performed for people who have been published in the journal. Telnet to e-math.ams.com and log in with the username and password 'e-math'. As of November 1993, the files used to produce the *Bulletin of the AMS* are available on E-Math for download or reading.

Colorado Alliance of Research Libraries (CARL)

The Colorado Alliance of Research Libraries (CARL), in association with CARL Systems, Inc., operates a public-access catalog of services. Offered are a number of library databases, including searches for government periodicals, book reviews, indices for current articles, and access to other library databases around the country. Other services are available only to CARL members, including an online encyclopedia and their UnCover database, which describes thousands of journals and their contents. Telnet to pac.carl.org, or write to 'help@carl.org' for more details.

Dartmouth Dante Project

Dartmouth College, in cooperation with Princeton University and the Dante Society of America, offers a unique service to literary scholars—the Dartmouth Dante Project. Telnet to library.dartmouth.edu, and at the prompt type 'connect dante'. The full text of Dante's *The Divine Comedy* ("La *Commedia*"), with over 600 years of commentary, can be examined using a sophisticated search engine. The system can be queried by a given term or terms, or by line—all references to a specified cantica (Inferno, Purgatorio, or Paradiso), canto, and line number will be returned. If you like, you can limit the results to a certain language (e.g., English, Latin, or Italian).

NASA/IPAC Extragalactic Database

The NASA/IPAC Extragalactic Database (NED) is an ongoing project, funded by NASA, to make data and literature on astronomical objects not belonging to our Milky Way galaxy available over computer networks. NED is an object-oriented database which contains extensive information for over 200,000 extragalactic objects taken from major catalogs of galaxies, quasars, and infrared and radio sources. NED provides positions, names, and other basic data (e.g., magnitude types, sizes, and redshifts) as well as bibliographic references and abstracts. Searches can be done by name, around a name, and by IAU shorthand. Search results can also be electronically mailed to the user. A tutorial is available that will guide a user through the retrieval process. Telnet to ned.ipac.caltech.edu and log in as 'ned'.

FEDIX—Minority Scholarship Information

FEDIX is an online information service that links the higher education community and the federal government to facilitate research, education, and services. The system provides accurate and timely federal agency information to colleges, universities, and other research organizations. There are no registration fees and no access charges for FEDIX whatsoever.

FEDIX offers the Minority On-Line Information Service (MOLIS), a database listing current information about African American and Latino colleges and universities.

Daily information updates are made on federal education and research programs, scholarships, fellowships, and grants, available used research equipment, and general information about FEDIX itself. To access the database, telnet to fedix.fie.com and log in as 'fedix'.

Clemson University Forestry and Agricultural Network

Clemson maintains a database similar to PENpages in content, but the information provided tends to be localized to the Southeastern United States. A menu-driven database offers queries involving the weather, food, family, and human resources. Telnet to eureka.clemson.edu and log in as 'PUBLIC'. You need to be on a good VT100 emulator (or a real VT terminal).

Geographic Name Server

A geographic database listing information for cities in the United States and some international locations is maintained by Tom Libert (libert@citi.umich.edu). The database is searchable by city name, zip code, etc. It will respond with a lot of information: the area code, elevation, time zone, and longitude and latitude are included. For example, a query of '95060' yields

```
0 Santa Cruz
1 06087 Santa Cruz
2 CA California
3 US United States
R county seat
F 45 Populated place
L 36 58 27 N 122 01 47 W
P 41483
E 17
Z 95060 95061 95062 95063 95064 95065 95066 .
```

To use the server, telnet to geoserver.eecs.umich.edu on port 3000. The command 'help' will yield further instructions, along with an explanation for each of the fields in a response.

Ham Radio Callbook

A callsign server was set up at the University at Buffalo by Devon Bowen, KA2NRC, to allow ham operators with Internet access to quickly find other hams without having to spend hours flipping through a paper callbook. The server, reached on port 2000 of callsign.cs.buffalo.edu, currently allows search by callsign, last name, city, or zip code. For information about the commands for the server, type 'help'.

The database for the server is based on the FCC (U.S.) tapes acquired by Rusty Carruth, N7IKQ, and a DOC (Canada) database obtained by Alan Paeth, VE3AWP, WA3YOK. The U.S. portion of the database has no clubs.

If you're interested in contributing to maintaining the database, contact Andrew Beers, N2LUH, of the University at Buffalo Ham Radio Club, either electronically at beers@cs.buffalo.edu or via snailmail to:

 SA – Amateur Radio Club
Re: The Callsign Project
111 Talbert Hall
State University of New York at Buffalo
Buffalo, NY 14260

The present maintainers accept any and all monetary donations to help keep the server available. A copy of the data is available from Andrew for $25. This purchase price pays for the data; any extra funds go to the club for equipment and activities.

University of Maryland Info Database

The Computer Science Center of the University of Maryland maintains a repository of information on a wide variety of topics—from computers to *Peter Pan*. They wish to give a working example of how network technology can (and should) provide as much information as possible to those who use it. Telnet to info.umd.edu and log in as 'info'. The information contained in the database is accessible through a very comfortable screen-oriented interface, and everything therein is available via anonymous FTP.

Comments and questions should go to 'info-editor@umail.-umd.edu'.

LawNet

The Columbia University Law School computer center runs "Law-Net," a resource for lawyers and legal researchers alike. You have access to the Columbia online law library Pegasus, full text searching of information on law firms, the U.S. courts, and other material, and a gateway into HYTELNET. Telnet to lawnet.law.columbia.edu and log in as 'lawnet'. If you have any trouble, write to their support staff at 'culawcc@lawmail.law.columbia.edu'.

Library of Congress

The Library of Congress in the United States has made a wealth of information available electronically. Their system, named LOCIS (the Library of Congress Information System), offers access to the entire Library of Congress catalog, information about federal legislation, searches on copyrights, and information about resources available from the Library of Congress for the blind and the deaf. Telnet to locis.loc.gov; type 'help' to learn how to use the different ways you can search their databases.

NASA SpaceLink

The Marshall Space Flight Center in Huntsville, Alabama, operates the NASA SpaceLink, a space-related informational database. Information on aeronautics, NASA news, NASA educational services, and the International Space Year (enacted by Congress to be 1992, the 500th anniversary of Columbus' Birthday) can be examined. Telnet to spacelink.msfc.nasa.gov and log in with 'NEWUSER' as the username and password. At any menu, type '?' to request additional information.

Net Mail Sites

Merit, Inc., provides a Net Mail Sites database to aid people in the search for a given university, company, or other network party. It maintains a database with Internet, UUCP, and BITNET host listings. Telnet to hermes.merit.edu and enter 'netmailsites' at main prompt. The system will ask you to enter the name of a site to search for, and respond with the mail information for each of the three major networks. Searching for "swarthmore", for example, yields:

```
:Enter the name of a site -> swarthmore
```

There are 3 sites found for SWARTHMORE

Internet Sites:
  CAMPUS.SWARTHMORE.EDU

Bitnet Sites:
  SWATPRM   Swarthmore College Computing Center - VAX

UUCP Sites:
  swatsun   Swarthmore College Computer Science Dept.

Some of the information for the Internet will be incomplete (e.g., searching for "widener" yields Widener University's old BITNET name and present UUCP name, but not any of its Internet names); nonetheless, using Net-mailsites is an excellent tool for finding addresses.

JVNCnet NICOL

JVNCnet offers information on JVNCnet, its members, and other Internet activities through the JVNCnet Network Information Center OnLine (NICOL). It also offers access to the Meckler MC(2) electronic information service (a valuable resource particularly to librarians). Write to 'meckler@jvnc.net' to subscribe to *MeckJournal*, the Meckler newsletter. To access NICOL, telnet to nicol.jvnc.net and log in as 'nicol'.

Ocean Network Information Center

The University of Delaware College of Marine Studies offers access to an interactive database of research information covering all aspects of marine studies, nicknamed OCEANIC. This includes the World Oceanic Circulation Experiment (WOCE) information and program information, research ship schedules and information, and a Who's Who of email and mailing addresses for oceanic studies. Data from a variety of academic institutions based _n research studies is also available. Telnet to delocn.udel.edu and log in as 'INFO'.

PENpages

PENpages is an agriculturally oriented database administered by Pennsylvania State University. Information entered into PENpages is provided by a number of sources, including the Pennsylvania Dept. of Agriculture, Rutgers University, and Penn State. Easy-to-use menus guide users to information ranging from cattle and agricultural prices to current weather information, from health information to agricultural news from around the nation. A keyword search option also allows users to search the database for related information and articles. The database is updated daily, and a listing of most recent additions is displayed after login. Telnet to psupen.psu.edu and log in as the user 'PNOTPA'.

Science and Technology Information System

The STIS is maintained by the National Science Foundation (NSF), and provides access to many NSF publications. The full text of publications can be searched online and copied from the system, which can accommodate up to ten users at one time. Telnet to stis.nsf.gov and log in as 'public'. Everything on the system is also available via anonymous FTP. For further information, contact:

STIS, Office of Information Systems, Room 401
National Science Foundation
1800 G. Street, N.W.
Washington, D.C. 20550
stis-request@nsf.gov
(202) 357-7492
(202) 357-7663 (Fax)

SuperNet

Advanced Networks & Services, Inc., maintains "SuperNet," an information search service. It offers a news service, information on the Internet (glossaries, RFCs, etc.), a Job Bank listing positions at business and academic institutions throughout the United States and overseas, newsletters such as *Vector Register* and *Dataquest Perspective*, and maintains six months of back issues of *Supercomputing Review* magazine—the latest volume is available at the end of each month. Telnet to super-net.ans.net and log in as 'supernet'.

Washington University Services

Washington University maintains a user-friendly gateway to many of the services listed in this section, along with many libraries and similar resources. You can choose which system to which to automatically connect by selecting from a well-organized menu of choices. Telnet to wugate.wustl.edu and log in as 'services' to try it out.

Weather Services

The University of Michigan's Department of Atmospheric, Oceanic, and Space Sciences maintains a database of weather and related information for the United States and Canada. Available are current weather conditions and forecasts for cities in the U.S. and Canada, a national weather summary, ski conditions, earthquake and hurricane updates, and a listing of severe weather conditions. Telnet to downwind.sprl.umich.edu on port 3000 to use the system.

The Atmospheric Science and Environmental Program at the University of Alabama at Huntsville also runs a weather server; telnet to wind.atmos.uah.edu on port 3000.

Bulletin Board Systems

There are a number of bulletin-board systems (BBSes) available on the Internet. Some are "traditional"—they're there for people to use conferences, have an interactive chat, and read local news announcements. Others were started for organizations to make information available to the general public, both through regular modem dial-up and over the Internet.

➡️ *Air Pollution*

The United States Environmental Protection Agency runs a BBS with information about air pollution, their policies, and other useful facts. Telnet to ttnbbs.rtpnc.epa.gov.

➡️ *American Philosophical Association*

The APA bulletin board includes information on the organization's regular proceedings, notices about grants, fellowships, and jobs, and APA members can send questions to the national office and submit short items for inclusion on the board. Telnet to eis.calstate.edu and log in as 'bbs'.

➡️ *Denver University*

In Colorado, Denver University has made available a bulletin board that offers its users email, Usenet news, and many other treats. You must have a notary public certify your registration, because the system was severely abused in its early days. Telnet to nyx.cs.du.edu and log in as 'new'.

➡️ *Food and Drug Administration*

The United States Food and Drug Administration started a bulletin board to make information about their policies, recent decisions, and regulations available to the public. Telnet to fdabbs.fda.gov and log in as 'bbs'.

➡️ *HP Calculators*

Users of the advanced Hewlett-Packard calculators can access a BBS that includes everything you would ever want to know about your calculator, and what you can do with it. Telnet to hpcvbbs.cv.hp.com and log in as 'new'.

➡ NIST Computer Security

The National Institute of Standards and Technology maintains a BBS to encourage the sharing of information that will help users and managers better protect their data and systems. Telnet to cs-bbs.ncsl.nist.gov; you will be brought through a registration process. A guide to using the BBS is available on csrc.ncsl.nist.gov in '/pub/nistir' as 'bbsguide.txt'.

➡ JewishNet

Members of the Jewish religion may talk to others about issues of the day, religious information, and other topics. Telnet to vms.huji.ac.il and log in as 'jewishnet'.

➡ Newton

A BBS for people teaching or studying science, math, or computer science is run by the Argonne National Laboratory in Argonne, Illinois. Telnet to newton.dep.anl.gov and log in as 'cocotext'.

➡ Rutgers University

The Quartz BBS at Rutgers has been one of the longest-lasting among Internet bulletin boards. It is often busy, but will give you pointers to other systems you can try in the meantime. Telnet to quartz.rutgers.edu and log in as 'bbs'.

"My consciousness suddenly switched locations, for the first time in my life, from the vicinity of my head and body to a point about twenty feet away from where I normally see the world."

— Howard Rheingold, *Virtual Reality*

➡ *UNC at Chapel Hill*

The University of North Carolina operates a very successful Internet BBS on launchpad.unc.edu; log in as 'launch'.

➡ *University of Iowa*

A popular BBS, called ISCA, is run at the University of Iowa. Telnet to bbs.isca.uiowa.edu and log in as 'guest'.

Information about new bulletin boards is often posted to the newsgroup alt.bbs.internet. Also, Scott Yanoff's list (see page 60) includes many BBSes in its collection of things you can try.

6 Various Tools

New and interesting ways to use the Internet are being dreamed up every day. As they gain widespread use, some methods become near-standard (or actual written-standard) Internet tools. A few are described in this chapter—there are undoubtedly others, and new ideas spring up all the time. An active user of the Internet will discover most of the more common ones in time. Usually, these services are free. See Chapter 7, *Commercial Services*, for applications that are commercially available over the Internet.

Usenet is often used to announce a new service or capability on the Internet. In particular, the groups comp.archives and alt.internet.services are good places to look. Information will drift into other areas as word spreads. Also, the InterNIC Info Scout (see page 95) will send you mail when new services and resources are announced.

Finger

On many systems there exists the 'finger' command, which provides information about each user that's currently logged in. This command also has extensions for use over the Internet, as well. Under normal circumstances, one would simply type 'finger' for a summary of who's logged into the local system, or 'finger *username*' for specific information about a user. It's also possible to go one step further and go onto the network:

finger @hostname

To see who is currently logged in at Widener University, for instance, use

```
% finger @cs.widener.edu
(cs.widener.edu)
Login          Name            TTY idle   When       Where
brendan        Brendan Kehoe   p0         Fri 02:14  tattoo.cs.widene
sven           Sven Heinicke   p1         Fri 04:16  xyplex3.cs.widen
```

To find out about a certain user, the user can be fingered specifically (and need not be logged in):

```
% finger bart@cs.widener.edu
(cs.widener.edu)
Login name: bart                      In real life: Bart Simpson
Directory: /home/springfield/bart     Shell: /bin/underachieve
Affiliation: Brother of Lisa          Home System: channel29.fox.org
Last login Thu May 23 12:14 (EDT) on ttyp6 from channel29.fox.org.
No unread mail
Project: To become a "fluff" cartoon character.
Plan:
Don't have a cow, man.
```

Please realize that some sites are very security-conscious, and need to restrict access to information about their systems and users. To that end, they often block finger requests from outside sites—so don't be surprised if fingering a computer or a user gives you the message 'Connection refused'.

There are a few systems that offer services by fingering a certain address; if you finger 'weather@synoptic.mit.edu', for example, you will find out if it's raining around MIT's Tech Square. The address 'quake@geophys.washington.edu' will offer information on earthquakes and other seismic data. By fingering 'nasanews-@space.mit.edu', you'll find out the latest in NASA Headline News. See page 95 for a description of a rather novel use of finger.

Ping

The 'ping' command allows the user to check if another system is currently "up" and running. The general form of the command is 'ping *system*'.[1] For example,

```
ping cs.widener.edu
```

will tell you if the main machine in Widener University's Computer Science lab is currently online. (They certainly hope so!)

Many implementations of 'ping' also include an option to let you see how fast a link is running (to give you some idea of the load on the network).

```
% ping -s cs.swarthmore.edu
PING cs.swarthmore.edu: 56 data bytes
64 bytes from 130.58.68.1: icmp_seq=0 ttl=251 time=66 ms
64 bytes from 130.58.68.1: icmp_seq=1 ttl=251 time=45 ms
64 bytes from 130.58.68.1: icmp_seq=2 ttl=251 time=46 ms
^C
--- cs.swarthmore.edu ping statistics ---
3 packets transmitted, 3 packets received, 0% packet loss
round-trip min/avg/max = 45/52/66 ms
```

This case tells us that for 'cs.swarthmore.edu', it takes about 46 milliseconds for a packet to go from Widener to Swarthmore College and back again. It also gives the average and worst-case speeds, and any packet loss that may have occurred (e.g., because of network congestion).

While 'ping' generally doesn't hurt network performance, you shouldn't use it *too* often—usually once or twice will leave you relatively sure of the other system's state.

Talk

Sometimes email is clumsy and difficult to manage when one really needs to have an interactive conversation. The Internet provides for that as well, in the form of *talk*. Two users can literally see each other type across thousands of miles.

1. The usage will, again, vary.

To talk with Bart Simpson at Widener, one would type

```
talk bart@cs.widener.edu
```

which would cause a message similar to the following to be displayed on Bart's terminal:

```
Message from Talk_Daemon@cs.widener.edu at 21:45 ...
talk: connection requested by joe@ee.someplace.edu
talk: respond with: talk joe@ee.someplace.edu
```

Bart would, presumably, respond by typing 'talk joe@ee.some-place.edu'. They could then chat about whatever they wished, with instantaneous response time, rather than the write-and-wait style of email. To leave talk, on many systems one would type Ctrl-C (hold down the Control key and press 'C'). Check local documentation to be sure.

There are two different versions of talk in common use today. The first, dubbed "old talk," is used by systems whose software hasn't been updated or revised in a while. The second, ntalk (aka "new talk"), is more of the standard. If, when attempting to talk with another user, the system responds with an error about protocol families, odds are the incompatibilities between versions of talk is the culprit. It's up to the system administrators of sites that use the old talk to install ntalk for their users.

Internet Navigation

When the Internet was still young, its creators faced a difficult challenge: how to make volumes of information available electronically. Finding space for all of the text, sound, and video that should be online was crucial. Since then, the price for storage has fallen dramatically. Also, the technology to convert printed text into electronic data is readily available to anyone who wants it in the form of optical character recognition (OCR) software.

As a direct result, there are now well over a billion bytes of raw information available for public consumption on the Internet. The issue has shifted from how to get all of the bits online, to how to navigate your way through such a glut of information to find what you really need.

Within a few months of each other, two new tools began to be used heavily on the Net. The first, the Wide Area Information Server (WAIS), lets you ask simple questions of a vast range of databases, covering all areas of interest from molecular biology to the Bible. The second, the Internet gopher, lets you walk your way through the Net, window shopping, until you discover what you're looking for.

Wide Area Information Server (WAIS)

One of the most powerful tools to appear in recent years has been the Wide Area Information Server (WAIS) system. (WAIS is pronounced "ways.") Started as a collaborative project between Thinking Machines, Dow Jones/News Retrieval, and Apple Computer, WAIS lets you search huge bodies of text in very little time.

The information in WAIS is divided into separate "sources"—there are well over 250 of them (so far), covering a wide range of topics. For example, you can search the King James version of the Bible for the phrase "burning bush," or look up synonyms for the word "travel" in a copy of *Roget's Thesaurus*.

There are a number of interfaces to WAIS—clients are available for the X-Window system, the NeXT, Macintoshes, and PCs. Similarly, there is a screen-based version (called swais) that lets you use WAIS on a normal terminal screen, rather than a fancy workstation. To try WAIS without using special local software, telnet to quake.think.com and log in as 'wais'. Each client (and the system you can telnet to) has online help to teach you what the keys and mouse selections will do.

The main idea behind WAIS is to let you search one or more of the sources for a given question (sometimes called a collection of keywords). If you ask WAIS the question "Tell me about DNA," and you select a few biology sources, you will likely get a number of *hits*, or matches, that include the information you were looking for. However, if you also select the source for movie reviews, included with all of the other matches, you will probably end up with a review of the movie *Jurassic Park*.

Since a question can end up giving you a lot of information you probably didn't expect, the result of a query is rated on a scale from 1 to 1000. A "score" of 1000 means a particular hit has a high likelihood of being what you were looking for. Likewise, a low score—say, 283—probably means the information in that hit won't be too useful, but it's included anyway, in case you need it.

The mailing list 'wais-discussion@think.com' is a periodic digest of messages about WAIS and similar issues; write to wais-discussion-request@think.com to subscribe. The list is also gatewayed into the Usenet newsgroup comp.infosystems.wais.

If you'd like to try the client software (your system administrator may need to install it for you), everything is available via anonymous FTP from the system ftp.cnidr.org.

The Internet Gopher

The students and staff of the University of Minnesota created a service called *gopher*, which lets you browse the Internet in a very comfortable and intuitive manner (burrowing your way under the Internet, to pop up where the information is, much like the cute and fuzzy gopher that keeps pestering your garden). Gopher makes it easy to access resources on the Internet in their many forms: as files to be transferred, services you telnet to, or WAIS databases you can search.

Since its first public introduction in December 1991, the total network traffic generated by gopher usage ballooned from 5 megabytes per month to over 100 gigabits per month in May of 1993. To put it another way, gopher really hit the ground running.

There are a number of ways to access gopher, ranging from a text-based interface for Unix, VMS, and DOS, to slick X-Window and Macintosh windowed clients. All of this software is available on the site boombox.micro.umn.edu in the directory '/pub/gopher'. If you don't have a local gopher client (try typing the command 'gopher' at your prompt), you can try it by telnetting to the system consultant.-micro.umn.edu and logging in as 'gopher'.

A typical gopher session presents you with an initial menu of things to look under. The default gopher server for the text-based clients (the original one at the University of Minnesota) presents you with these selections:

```
Internet Gopher Information Client 2.0 pl6

Root gopher server: gopher.tc.umn.edu

--> 1. Information About Gopher/
    2. Computer Information/
    3. Discussion Groups/
    4. Fun & Games/
    5. Internet file server (ftp) sites/
    6. Libraries/
    7. News/
    8. Other Gopher and Information Servers/
    9. Phone Books/
   10. Search Gopher Titles at the University of Minnesota <?>
   11. Search lots of places at the University of Minnesota <?>
   12. University of Minnesota Campus Information/

Press ? for Help, q to Quit, u to go up a menu    Page: 1/1
```

Each entry in the list is of a specific type; for example, a trailing slash ('/') at the end means that there is other information beneath an entry. The symbol '<TEL>' after an entry means it's something you will telnet to (gopher will tell you what account you need to log in with, if any), and '<?>' means it's something you can search, like a WAIS index or a database of movie reviews.

You hit the RETURN key to move down into another area, and use the 'u' key to move back up. In the previous menu, if you were to hit RETURN on "News", you'd see a new menu of things related to different kinds of news:

```
Internet Gopher Information Client 2.0 pl6


News

--> 1. Cornell Chronicle (Weekly)/
    2. French Language Press Review/
```

3. Minnesota Daily/
4. NASA News.
5. National Weather Service Forecasts/
6. Other Newspapers, Magazines, and Newsletters /
7. Technolog (Institute of Technology, University of
   Minnesota)/
8. The Daily Illini (University of Illinois)/
9. The Gazette (University of Waterloo)/
10. UPI News/
11. USENET News (from Michigan State)/
12. University of Minnesota News (U Relations)/

Press ? for Help, q to Quit, u to go up a menu Page: 1/1

Finally, if you hit RETURN on "NASA News", it will retrieve the file for you and let you read it. You'll have an opportunity to mail the file to yourself (or someone else's email address) or save it into a file.

The Usenet newsgroup comp.infosystems.gopher was created for discussions about gopher. The maintainers of the gopher software announce new releases there, and people can ask experienced gopher users for help with problems they've encountered in browsing Gopher-Space.

Learning to work your way through GopherSpace is very easy, regardless of which kind of client you happen to be using. Those written for windowing systems (like the X-Window system) are particularly easy—you just point and click on what you want to look at. You're encouraged to walk around for a bit, to get a feel for what kind of things are hidden inside of gopher. Then, when you begin to wonder how in the world you might find something on, say, archaeology, try using Veronica.

Veronica

As "GopherSpace" grew, it became difficult to find things quickly with gopher. The number of new servers grew at a phenomenal rate; subsequently, the information you're looking for might be buried fifteen levels down an obscure path.

The staff at the University of Nevada Reno had a brilliant idea—create a tool that will itself help you find things inside of gopher. It took the form of *veronica*[2] a searchable node in gopherspace. By selecting 'Other Gopher and Information Servers/' from the main gopher node, you can then opt to search titles in GopherSpace with veronica.

A query of "archaeology" can yield more than fifty hits. While veronica did help you find all of the areas inside of gopher that had to do with archaeology, the search is a raw one—as you make your way down the list, going through what you were able to find, odds are that a number of the matches will end up being things like Departments of Archaeology at various learning institutions around the world. However, in all likelihood, at least one of the matches will include a wealth of information, including what you originally set out to find.

As a final note, the name "veronica" stands for—take a deep breath—Very Easy Rodent-Oriented Net-wide Index to Computerized Archives. All hail the mighty acronym, it hath struck again.

Netfind: Finding Your Friends

The scope of the Internet often makes it difficult to find the people you want to contact. Michael Schwartz, a professor at the University of Colorado at Boulder, has developed a tool called *netfind* as part of his research on Internet resource discovery.[3] Given the name of the person you're looking for and a rough description of where the person might be (the name of their University or work place, for example), netfind will go out onto the Net and try to find out information about them. It uses a range of methods, from mail-based information to using finger and the domain name system.

A netfind query might look like "poulson widener university". The first field is the name of the person you're looking for, and subsequent fields are to help netfind make some intelligent guesses about where they might be. The word "university" is a clue that the domain for

---

2. The name "veronica" is a play on the name of "archie," characters in the popular comic strip *Archie*.

3. The work that Professor Schwartz has been doing—including measuring the average reachability of hosts on the Internet—makes for fascinating reading. His papers are available on ftp.cs.colorado.edu in the directory '/pub/cs/techreports/schwartz'.

the place "widener" will very possibly be in the edu domain. The system will next look for domain names that might match widener, and find the domain widener.edu.

By using standard mail commands (based on the SMTP standard, not on the user command mail) and finger, netfind will likely help you find the address for Joshua Poulson at Widener University.

There are a number of netfind servers around the world; if you telnet to bruno.cs.colorado.edu or netfind.oc.com and log in as 'netfind', you'll be given a list of other netfind servers that can be used. It's suggested that you *not* use the one at Colorado, since it tends to be heavily loaded. There is also an extensive offering of online help (along with a more detailed explanation of how netfind works) available from the main netfind menu.

The WHOIS Database

The main WHOIS database is run by the Registration Services part of the InterNIC (see page 95). The 'whois' command will let you search a database of every registered domain (e.g., 'mit.edu') and of registered users. It's primarily used by system postmasters or listowners for finding the *Points of Contact* for a site, to let them know of a problem or contact them for one reason or another. You can also find out their postal address. If we were trying to reach MIT's main network contact, for example, we might use:

```
% whois mit.edu
Massachusetts Institute of Technology (MIT) MIT.EDU     18.72.2.1
   Massachusetts Institute of Technology (MIT-DOM)          MIT.EDU
```

Note that there are two entries for 'mit.edu'; we'll go for the second. Entries with a '-DOM' suffix usually contain the most complete record of information for a domain.

```
% whois mit-dom
Massachusetts Institute of Technology (MIT-DOM) ) Mailing address
   Cambridge, MA 02139
```

```
Domain Name: MIT.EDU => Domain name

Administrative Contact, Technical Contact, Zone Contact:
  Schiller, Jeffrey I.   (JIS) JIS@MIT.EDU
  (617) 253-8400

Record last updated on 22-Jun-88.  ➥ Last change made to the record

Domain servers in listed order: ➥ Systems that can tell you the
                                        Internet addresses for a site
STRAWB.MIT.EDU                  18.71.0.151
W20NS.MIT.EDU                   18.70.0.160
BITSY.MIT.EDU                   18.72.0.3
LITHIUM.LCS.MIT.EDU             18.26.0.121

To see this host record with registered users, repeat the command with a star
('*') before the name; or, use '%' to show JUST the registered users.
```

Much better! Now this information (sought, possibly, by a system administrator) can be used to find out how to notify MIT of a security issue or problem with connectivity.

Note that as of April 1, 1993, the old WHOIS server nic.ddn.mil only provides information about people and organizations in the United States Department of Defense (on the Milnet). If the whois command on your system still sends queries to nic.ddn.mil, and not the new WHOIS server whois.internic.net, your support staff or system supplier should be contacted for an updated whois program.

Other Uses of WHOIS

Many educational sites run WHOIS servers of their own, to offer information about people who may be currently on the staff or attending the institution. To specify a WHOIS server, many implementations include some sort of option or qualifier—in VMS under MultiNet, it's '/HOST', in Unix the '-h' command-line switch. To receive information about using the Stanford server from a Unix system, one might use the command 'whois -h stanford.edu help'.

A large list of systems offering WHOIS services is being maintained by Matt Power of MIT (mhpower@athena.mit.edu). It is available via anonymous FTP from sipb.mit.edu, in the directory 'pub/whois'. The file is named 'whois-servers.list'.

Included on the list are Syracuse University (syr.edu), New York University (acfcluster.nyu.edu), the University of California at San Diego (ucsd.edu), and Stanford University (stanford.edu).

"Fingers were made before forks."

— Jonathan Swift, *Polite Conversation*

7 Commercial Services

Many services can be accessed through the Internet. As time progresses and more outlets for commercial activity appear, once-restricted traffic (by the NSFnet Acceptable Use Policy) may now flow freely. Now that there are other networks for that information to travel on, businesses are making their move.

Electronic Journals

The Association of Research Libraries (ARL) publishes a hard-copy directory of electronic journals, newsletters, and scholarly discussion lists. Written by Michael Strangelove, the directory is a compilation of entries for hundreds of scholarly lists, dozens of journals and newsletters, and many "other" titles, including newsletter-digests, into one reference source. Each entry includes instructions for accessing the referenced publication or list.

The documents are available electronically by sending the commands

```
get ejournl1 directry
get ejournl2 directry
```

to the server at 'LISTSERV@UOTTAWA.BITNET'. See page 16 for further instructions on using a listserv.

The directory, along with a compilation by Diane Kovacs called *Directories of Academic E-Mail Conferences*, is available in print and on diskette (DOS WordPerfect and MacWord) from:

Office of Scientific & Academic Publishing
Association of Research Libraries
1527 New Hampshire Avenue, NW
Washington, DC 20036
ARLHQ@UMDC.BITNET
(202) 232-2466
(202) 462-7849 (Fax)

The ARL is a not-for-profit organization representing over 100 research libraries in the United States and Canada. The publication is available to ARL members for $10 and to non-members for $20 (add $5 postage per directory for foreign addresses). Orders of six or more copies will receive a 10% discount; all orders must be prepaid and sent to the ARL.

ClariNet News

ClariNet is a for-profit electronic publishing network service that provides professional news and information, including live UPI wire service news.

ClariNet lets you read an "electronic newspaper" right on the local system; you can get timely industry news, technology-related wirestories, syndicated columns and features, financial information, stock quotes, and more.

The main distribution mechanism for ClariNet is through a collection of Usenet newsgroups whose names begin with 'clari'. Your system, if it is a subscriber, can receive a feed either directly from ClariNet, or from any other news server whose organization is also a subscriber to the service.

The main feature is *ClariNews*, an "electronic newspaper," gathered live from the wire services of United Press International (UPI). Clari–News articles are distributed in 100 newsgroups based on their subject matter, and are keyworded for additional topics and the geographical location of the story. ClariNews includes headlines, industry news, box scores, network TV schedules, and more. The main products of ClariNews are:

- *ClariNews General,* the general news "paper" with news, sports, and features, averaging about 400 stories per day.

- *TechWire,* special groups for stories on science, technology, and industry stories around them.

- *ClariNews-Biz,* business and financial stories.

- *Newsbytes,* a daily computer-industry news magazine.

- *Syndicated Columns,* including Dave Barry (humor) and Mike Royko (opinion).

For full information on ClariNet, including subscription information, contact:

ClariNet Communications Corp.
Box 1479
Cupertino, CA 95015
info@clarinet.com
(800) USE-NETS in the United States
(408) 296-0366 elsewhere

Also, the directory '/ClariNet' on ftp.uu.net gives the details on the assortment of services they provide.

Bunyip Information Services

Bunyip Information Systems Incorporated was formed in January 1992 to create and market a range of network-based tools and information services. The company is a world leader in the research and deployment of innovative technology for the developing Internet marketplace, marketing the successful archie information distribution system product (already licensed to over 30 sites around the world) as well as contributing numerous technical advances in this fast-changing and highly specialized field. (See page 29 for instructions on how to access their archie servers.)

Their first product, the well-known archie system, provides a practical method for distributing information to the fast-growing commercial Internet market. archie was first deployed in 1991 and has been continually enhanced throughout the past two years. Further information distribution services based upon this software have been developed and are scheduled to begin operations in late 1993.

Using their technology and working with representatives from the publishing industry, they created an information distribution mechanism capable of providing authenticated, controlled access to high-quality information across the Internet. Services based upon this technology will distribute collections of books, articles, and other commercial-quality information, all supplemented with a range of computer-enhanced value-added services using a simple subscription-based revenue model.

The founders of Bunyip Information Systems developed the archie information distribution system, the first Internet-based information indexing and distribution service. The archie software is now licensed by over 30 commercial and academic sites around the world and has proven to be a tremendous success on the Internet. The system has demonstrated the power of information systems in an Internet environment and the value of commercial versions of those programs. Bunyip also provides technical consulting and develops tutorials and documentation.

You can reach the folks at Bunyip by writing or calling:

Bunyip Information Services
310 Ste-Catherine St. W, Suite 202
Montreal, Quebec
CANADA H2X 2A1
info@bunyip.com
(514) 875-8611
(514) 875-8134 (Fax)

Commercial Databases

The American Institute of Physics maintains the Physics Information Network. It contains the bibliographic SPIN and General Physics Advanced Abstracts databases. Also available is access to bulletin boards and several searchable lists (job notices, announcements, etc.). Telnet to pinet.aip.org; new users should log in as 'new', with a password of 'new' to register.

Online Services

Traditional commercial online services, like CompuServe, have recognized that many of their users also have access to the Internet from home, work, or school, and would find it useful to be able to access their accounts through the Internet. In answer to this, it's now possible to access CompuServe, BIX, and GEnie using telnet.

To connect to BIX, simply type

```
telnet bix.com
```

and log in as you normally would. Note that a small surcharge will be applied to your BIX account for logging in through the Internet.

For CompuServe, connect to hermes.merit.edu and select 'compuserve' as the service:

```
% telnet hermes.merit.edu
Trying 35.1.48.167 ...
Connected to hermes.merit.edu.
Escape character is '^)'.

%Merit:Hermes (HME777:TN02:VT100:EDIT=MTS)
%You have reached MichNet, operated by Merit Network, Inc.
%Enter a destination, or enter HELP for assistance.

Which Host?compuserve
%TN02:HME777-AB2F:TE00 compus
%Call connected

User ID:
```

Starting with the 'User ID:' prompt, you are connected to CompuServe and should proceed as you would dialing CompuServe directly with a modem. Do note, however, that CompuServe does charge an extra fee to your account for these connections—contact the customer service department at CompuServe for the details.

Finally, to connect to GEnie, use the same method as above for connecting to CompuServe, but at the 'Which Host?' prompt, type

Which Host? *sprintnet-313171*

Again, there will be a surcharge to your GEnie account for using this method; call their customer service department to find out the details.

"Needless to say, Aristotle did not envisage modern finance."

— Frederick Copleston, S.J.
A History of Philosophy, v.1

8 Things You'll Hear About

There are certain things that you'll hear about shortly after you start actively using the Internet. Most people assume that everyone's familiar with them, and that they require no additional explanation. If only this were true!

This section addresses a few topics that are commonly encountered and asked about as a new user explores Cyberspace. Some of them are directly related to how the networks are run today; other points are simply interesting to read about.

The Internet Worm

On November 2, 1988, Robert T. Morris, then a graduate student in computer science at Cornell, wrote a self-replicating, self-propagating program called a *worm* and injected it into the Internet. Morris soon discovered that the program was replicating and reinfecting machines at a much faster rate than he had anticipated—there was a bug. Experts also believe that Morris didn't fully understand the reasoning behind what he was attempting. Ultimately, many machines at locations around the country either crashed or became "catatonic." When Morris realized what was happening, he contacted a friend at Harvard to discuss a solution. Eventually, they sent an anonymous message from Harvard over the network, instructing programmers on how to prevent reinfection. However, because the network route was clogged, this message did not get through until it was too late. Computers were affected at many sites, including universities, military sites, and medical research facilities. The estimated cost of dealing with the worm at each installation ranged from $200 to more than $53,000.

The worm took advantage of three weaknesses then present in Unix systems. First, many sites left a debugging option enabled in the network mail agent, *sendmail,* that allowed an outside user to issue privileged commands. Also, a problem with the finger daemon, *fingerd,* which serves finger requests (see page 75), allowed the worm to introduce commands to be executed by giving *fingerd* too much information. Finally, the everpresent problem of users choosing poor passwords was vital to the worm's existence—given a limited dictionary of words and common names (like those of possible girlfriends), it could find an impressive number of passwords.

People at the University of California at Berkeley, MIT, and Purdue, to name just a few, had copies of the program and were actively *disassembling* it (returning the program back into its source form) to try to figure out how it worked. Teams of programmers worked nonstop to come up with at least a temporary fix, to prevent the continued spread of the worm. After about twelve hours, the team at Berkeley came up with steps that would help retard the spread of the program. Another method was also discovered at Purdue and widely published. The information didn't get out as quickly as it could have, however, because so many sites had completely disconnected themselves from the network.

After a few days things slowly began to return to normalcy, and everyone wanted to know *who* had done it all. Morris later admitted to John Markoff of *The New York Times* that he was the author, after Markoff received an anonymous tip. Investigation later found sufficient evidence to indict him. In the interim, he was expelled from Cornell.

Robert T. Morris was convicted of a felony under the Computer Fraud and Abuse Act (Title 18 of the United States Code, section 1030). He was sentenced, in May 1990, to three years of probation, 400 hours of community service, a fine of $10,050, and the costs of his supervision—his sentencing was outside of Federal guidelines that suggested a mandatory period of incarceration. His conviction was upheld by the Circuit Court of Appeals, and the Supreme Court declined to hear the case. He is currently working as a programmer (on non-security-related projects) for a Boston-area software company.

A Coke Machine on the Internet?

 Since time immemorial (well, maybe 1970), the Carnegie-Mellon Computer Science Department has maintained a departmental Coke machine, which sells bottles of Coke for a dime or so less than other vending machines around campus. As no Real Programmer can function without caffeine, the machine is very popular. (It reportedly had the highest sales volume of any Coke machine in the Pittsburgh area.) The machine is loaded on a rather erratic schedule by grad student volunteers.[1]

In the mid-'70s, expansion of the department caused people's offices to be located ever further away from the main terminal room where the Coke machine stood. It got rather annoying to traipse down to the third floor only to find the machine empty; or worse, to shell out hard-earned cash to receive a recently loaded, still-warm Coke. One day a couple of people got together to devise a solution.

They installed microswitches in the Coke machine to sense how many bottles were present in each of its six columns of bottles. The switches were hooked up to CMUA, the PDP-10 that was then the main departmental computer. A server program was written to keep tabs on the Coke machine's state, including how long each bottle had been in the machine. When you ran the companion status inquiry program, you'd get a display that might look like:

```
EMPTY  EMPTY 1h 3m
COLD   COLD  1h 4m
```

1. Thanks to Tom Lane (tom_lane@g.gp.cs.cmu.edu) for this fantastic anecdote.

This lets you know that cold Coke could be had by pressing the lower-left or lower-center button, while the bottom bottles in the two right-hand columns had been loaded an hour or so beforehand, so were still warm. (The display changed to just "COLD" after the bottle had been there several hours. The server actually kept track of each bottle's state, though it would only tell you about the bottommost bottle in each column.)

The final piece of the puzzle was needed to let people check Coke status when they were logged in on machines other than CMUA. CMUA's finger server was modified to run the Coke status program whenever someone fingered the nonexistent user 'coke' (see page 75 for more on finger). Since finger requests are part of standard Internet protocols, people could check the Coke machine from any CMU computer with the command 'finger coke@cmua'. In fact, you could discover the Coke machine's status from any machine anywhere on the Internet! Not that it would do you much good if you were a few thousand miles away.

Nothing similar has been done elsewhere, so CMU can legitimately boast of having the only Coke machine on the Internet. (MIT can claim priority on having a computerized Coke machine, but theirs wasn't hooked up to Internet protocols.)

The Coke machine programs were used for over a decade, and were even rewritten for Unix Vaxen when CMUA was retired in the early '80s. The end came in the late '80s, when the local Coke bottler discontinued the returnable, Coke-bottle-shaped bottles. The old machine couldn't handle the nonreturnable, totally-uninspired-shape bottles, so it was replaced by a new vending machine. This was right after the New Coke fiasco; the combination of these events left CMU Coke lovers sufficiently disgruntled that no one has bothered to wire up the new machine.

The Cuckoo's Egg

 First in an article entitled "Stalking the Wily Hacker," and later in the book *The Cuckoo's Egg*, Clifford Stoll described his experiences trying to track down an intruder on a system at the Lawrence Berkeley Laboratory, located in Berkeley, California.[2]

A 75-cent discrepancy in the Lab's accounting records led Stoll on a chase through California, Virginia, and Europe to end up in a small apartment in Hannover, West Germany. Stoll dealt with many levels of bureaucracy and red tape, and worked with the FBI, the CIA, and the German Bundespost trying to track his hacker down.

The experiences of Stoll, and particularly his message in speaking engagements, have all pointed out the dire need for communication between parties on a network of networks. The only way everyone can peacefully coexist in Cyberspace is by ensuring rapid recognition of any existing problems.

Organizations

 The indomitable need for humans to congregate and share their common interests is ever-present in the computing world. *User groups* exist around the world, where people share ideas and experiences. Similarly, there are organizations that are one step "above" user groups; that is to say, they exist to encourage or promote an idea or set of ideas, rather than to support a specific computer or application of computers.

The Association for Computing Machinery

The Association for Computing Machinery (ACM) was founded in 1947, immediately after Eckert and Mauchly unveiled one of the first electronic computers, the ENIAC, in 1946. Since then, the ACM has grown by leaps and bounds, becoming one of the leading educational and scientific societies in the computer industry.

2 See the bibliography for full citations.

The ACM's stated purposes are:

- To advance the sciences and arts of information processing;

- To promote the free interchange of information about the sciences and arts of information processing both among specialists and among the public;

- To develop and maintain the integrity and competence of individuals engaged in the practices of the sciences and arts of information processing.

Membership in the ACM has grown from 78 in September 1947, to over 77,000 today. There are local chapters around the world, and many colleges and universities endorse student chapters. Lecturers frequent these meetings, which tend to be one step above the normal "user group" gathering. A large variety of published material is also available at discounted prices for members of the association.

The ACM has a number of *Special Interest Groups* (SIGs) that concentrate on certain areas of computing, ranging from graphics to the Ada programming language to security. Each of the SIGs also publishes its own newsletter. There is a Usenet group, `comp.org.acm`, for the discussion of ACM topics. See Chapter 4, *Usenet News*, for more information on reading news.

For more information and a membership application, write to:

Association for Computing Machinery
1515 Broadway
New York City, NY 10036
ACMHELP@ACMVM.BITNET
(212) 869-7440

Computer Professionals for Social Responsibility

CPSR is an alliance of computer professionals concentrating on certain areas of the impact of computer technology on society. It traces its history to the Fall of 1981, when several researchers in Palo Alto, California, organized a lunch meeting to discuss their shared concerns about the connection between computing and the nuclear arms race. Out of that meeting and the discussions which followed, CPSR was born, and has been active ever since.[3]

The national CPSR program focuses on the following project areas:

- *Reliability and Risk* This area reflects on the concern that over-reliance on computing technology can lead to unacceptable risks to society. It includes, but isn't limited to, work in analyzing military systems such as SDI.

- *Civil Liberties and Privacy* This project is concerned with such topics as the FBI National Crime Information Center, the growing use of databases by both government and private industry, the right of access to public information, extension of First Amendment rights to electronic communication, and establishing legal protections for privacy of computerized information.

- *Computers in the Workplace* The CPSR Workplace Project has concentrated its attention on the design of software for the workplace, and particularly on the philosophy of "participatory design," in which software designers work together with users to ensure that systems meet the actual needs of that workplace.

- *The 21st Century Project* This is a coalition with other professional organizations working towards redirecting national research priorities from concentrating on military issues to anticipating and dealing with future problems as science and technology enter the next century.

For more information on the CPSR, contact them at:

 Computer Professionals for Social Responsibility
P.O. Box 717
Palo Alto, CA 94302
cpsr@csli.stanford.edu
(415) 322-3778
(415) 322-3798 (Fax)

---

3. This section is part of the CPSR's letter to prospective members.

The Electronic Frontier Foundation

The Electronic Frontier Foundation (EFF) was established to help civilize the "electronic frontier"—the Cyberspacial medium becoming ever-present in today's society; to make it truly useful and beneficial not just to a technical elite, but to everyone; and to do this in a way that is in keeping with the society's highest traditions of the free and open flow of information and communication.

The mission of the EFF is

- to engage in and support educational activities that increase popular understanding of the opportunities and challenges posed by developments in computing and telecommunications;

- to develop among policy-makers a better understanding of the issues underlying free and open telecommunications, and support the creation of legal and structural approaches that will ease the assimilation of these new technologies by society;

- to raise public awareness about civil liberties issues arising from the rapid advancement in the area of new computer-based communications media and, where necessary, support litigation in the public interest to preserve, protect, and extend First Amendment rights within the realm of computing and telecommunications technology;

- to encourage and support the development of new tools that will endow non-technical users with full and easy access to computer-based telecommunications.

The Usenet newsgroups comp.org.eff.talk and comp.org.eff.news are dedicated to discussion concerning the EFF. They also have mailing list counterparts for those that don't have access to Usenet, 'eff-talk-request@eff.org' and 'eff-news-request@eff.org'. The first is an informal arena (aka a normal newsgroup) where anyone may voice his or her opinions. The second, comp.org.eff.news, is a moderated area for regular postings from the EFF in the form of *EFFector Online*. To submit a posting for the *EFFector Online*, or to get general information about the EFF, write to 'eff@eff.org'. There is also a wealth of information available via anonymous FTP on ftp.eff.org.

The EFF can be contacted at

The Electronic Frontier Foundation, Inc.
1001 G Street, NW
Suite 950 East
Washington, DC 20001
eff@eff.org
(202) 347-5400
(202) 393-5509 (Fax)

The Free Software Foundation

The Free Software Foundation was started by Richard M. Stallman (creator of the popular GNU Emacs editor). It is dedicated to eliminating restrictions on copying, redistributing, and modifying software.

The word "free" in their name does not refer to price; it refers to freedom: first, the freedom to copy a program and redistribute it to your neighbors, so that they can use it as well as you; and second, the freedom to change a program, so that you can control it instead of it controlling you; for this, the source code must be made available to you.

The Foundation works to provide these freedoms by developing free compatible replacements for proprietary software. Specifically, they are putting together a complete, integrated software system called "GNU" that is upward-compatible with Unix.[4] When it is released, everyone will be permitted to copy it and distribute it to others. In addition, it will be distributed with source code, so you will be able to learn about operating systems by reading it, to port it to your own machine, and to exchange the changes with others.

---

4. As an aside, the editor of the GNU project, e m a c s, contains a built-in LISP interpreter, and a large part of its functionality is written in LISP. The name GNU is itself *recursive* (the mainstay of the LISP language); it stands for "Gnu's Not Unix."

For more information on the Free Software Foundation and the status of the GNU Project, or for a list of the current tasks that still need to be done, write to gnu@prep.ai.mit.edu. The software produced by the GNU Project is on prep.ai.mit.edu in '/pub/gnu'; it includes most of the standard Unix utilities, compilers for the C and C++ languages, a debugger, and many other useful tools.[5]

The Internet Society

In January 1992, the Internet Society was formed to promote the use of the Internet for research and scholarly communication and collaboration. As a non-profit organization, the Society hopes to:

■ facilitate and support the technical evolution of the Internet as a research and education infrastructure, and to stimulate the involvement of the scientific community, industry, and the public at large;

■ to educate the scientific community, industry, and the public at large concerning the technology, use, and application of the Internet;

■ to promote educational applications of the Internet technology for the benefit of government, colleges and universities, industry, and the public at large;

■ to provide a forum for exploration of new Internet applications, and to stimulate collaboration among organizations in their operational use of the global Internet.

Membership is inexpensive and open to anyone; organizations are strongly urged to join. All organizational members receive discounts for selected Society functions and services, complimentary copies of Society publications, and an opportunity to designate a representative to the Internet Society Advisory Council. More information and applications are available from

---

5. A company, Cygnus Support, was founded to provide commercial support for free software, including many of the development tools distributed by the FSF. Write info@cygnus.-com' for information on their services.

The Internet Society
1895 Preston White Drive, Suite 100
Reston, VA 22091
isoc@isoc.org

The League for Programming Freedom

The League for Programming Freedom is a grass-roots organization of professors, students, businessmen, programmers, and users dedicated to "bringing back" the freedom to write programs, which they contend has been lost over the past number of years. The League is not opposed to the legal system that Congress intended—copyright on individual programs. Their aim is to reverse the recent changes made by judges in response to special interests, often explicitly rejecting the public-interest principles of the Constitution.

The League works to abolish the new monopolies by publishing articles, talking with public officials, boycotting egregious offenders, and in the future possibly intervening in court cases. On May 24, 1989, the League picketed Lotus headquarters because of their lawsuits, and then again on August 2, 1990. These marches stimulated widespread media coverage for the issue. They welcome suggestions for other activities, as well as help in carrying them out.

For information on the League and how to join, write to

League for Programming Freedom
1 Kendall Square #143
P.O. Box 9171
Cambridge, MA 02139
league@uunet.uu.net

Also, the system prep.ai.mit.edu houses information on patents and the LPF in the directory '/pub/lpf'.

The Society for Electronic Access

While the Internet is gaining more acceptance among people who are not "techno-wizards" or have to use it as part of their daily work, the amount of information involved in using the Net can have a chilling effect upon its success. While more exposure in the general media does help, crossing class boundaries and making "Cyberspace a better place to live, work, and visit" is not yet a fully realized goal.

The Society for Electronic Access was formed in 1992 by Simona Nass (with some friends) to work towards accomplishing that goal. Its membership is an excellent cross section of society, from the interested public to lawyers, journalists to librarians. They work to make information about legislative computer and telecommunications policy more readily available, and educate the general public about the Net in general (e.g., how to access and use electronic mail). In addition, media coverage of the Net is tracked by the Society, to aid journalists in researching and developing articles in related areas.

In the past, legislators have declined the opportunity to have constituents reach them through email, for the most part because they don't understand exactly what is involved. The SEA is a valuable resource for these lawmakers; the accurate and useful information the Society provides can help lead to a more informed decision. As the Internet grows in popularity and accessibility, legislators will find that Cyberspace is an even more powerful medium than the conventional telephone or postal service.

Membership in the SEA is open to anyone interested in helping them achieve their goals. The primary means of discussion among SEA members is via electronic mailing lists, but you don't have to have email access to become a member. There are a number of working groups in the Society addressing issues ranging from the legal aspects of Cyberspace to how the media is presenting the Net to the world.

To contact the Society for Electronic Access, write to

 The Society for Electronic Access
180 Thompson St. 1D
New York, NY 10012
sea-info@sea.org
(212) 592-3801

The InterNIC

 In January 1993, the NSFnet made a significant step forward in the evolution of the Internet as a coherent body. In the past, the NSFnet Network Service Center (NNSC) was the single point of contact for people seeking information about the Internet, from the very basic to the highly technical. To replace it, the NSFnet created a new triumvirate, collectively known as the "InterNIC." Three separate companies were awarded contracts to offer three distinct areas of support for the Internet. The new InterNIC began operation on April 1, 1993.

The Registration Services area of the InterNIC, provided by Network Solutions, is responsible for keeping track of Internet numbers so they don't get repeated, register new domain names, and keep track of contacts for those domains. They also maintain the WHOIS database (see page 84 for details on using whois).

The Directory and Database Services area, provided by AT&T, maintains the *Directory of Directories* (see Chapter 9, *Finding Out More*). They maintain a number of databases, and operate a gopher server. To find out more, write 'admin@ds.internic.net' or call (908) 668-6587.

Finally, General Atomics supplies the Information Services work for the InterNIC. They offer training classes and documentation, a Reference Desk people can call with questions, and work to coordinate the many networks that compose the Internet. They also have an Info Scout, a service which notifies people when new resources are announced on the Net. Write to 'listserv@is.internic.net' with

subscribe net-resources *Your Name*

in the body of the message. You will receive periodic messages from the Info Scout about newly announced tools and services available on the Internet.

The new Reference Desk is a very encouraging development. Now anyone using the Internet can call with questions and receive either an immediate answer, or a referral to someone who can help. They also provide information on how to get connected (see (undefined), *Hooking Up* for some information along these lines). You can reach the Reference Desk by writing or calling

InterNIC Information Services
General Atomics
P.O. Box 85608
San Diego, CA 92186-9784
info@internic.net
(800) 444-4345 in the United States
(619) 455-4600 outside of the US
(619) 455-3990 (Fax)

The White House

In 1993, the White House Communications Office announced that for the first time in history, the leaders of a major world power would be reachable through Cyberspace. The President and Vice President of the United States have electronic mail addresses:

president@whitehouse.gov
vice.president@whitehouse.gov

Direct replies from them aren't possible yet—the sheer volume of mail that goes to those two addresses is more than a single person could possibly hope to wade through. Instead, your message will be sorted, and a reply will come through the conventional postal service.

In addition, press releases and other documents are regularly posted to the Usenet newsgroups alt.politics.usa.misc, alt.news-media, and talk.politics.misc, among others. The White House also has a strong presence on a variety of commercial online services, including CompuServe, America Online, and MCI Mail.

If you'd like to receive White House press releases via email, write to the address 'Clinton-Info@Campaign92.Org'. In the 'Subject:'

header, just include the word 'help'. The White House mail server will return instructions describing how to receive all of the press releases, or only those concerning certain topics (e.g., the economy, foreign policy, etc.). If you'd like more detailed help, send your mail as

```
To: Clinton-Info@Campaign92.Org
Subject: Please Help!
```

Also, all of this information is available via anonymous FTP from a number of sites, including sunsite.unc.edu in the directory

```
pub/academic/political-science/whitehouse-papers
```

and from cpsr.org in '/cpsr/clinton'. Finally, you can search the White House papers through gopher (see page 80 to learn how to use gopher) by using the gopher server on sunsite.unc.edu, in the "Politics" area. If you don't have a gopher client, telnet to sunsite.unc.edu and log in as 'gopher' (it won't ask you for a password).

MTV on the Internet

In late 1993, Adam Curry, a video-jockey (VJ) on MTV, registered mtv.com as a domain on the Internet. It offers "one-stop" shopping for entertainment, in the form of daily Cyber-Sleaze reports, Quicktime movies, audio, and many other things. Information on artists and things going on with MTV will also be offered. Items available via anonymous FTP are available on ftp.mtv.com. They run a gopher server (on mtv.com) which will include the FTPable items, plus pointers to other Net resources that are of similar interest to their audience.

Text Projects

The wealth of information available to modern researchers is frequently overwhelming—months can be spent in a library trying to track down a few disparate facts. The advent of computers has spurred the development of projects to make books and other information available electronically, thus dramatically reducing the time needed to search for information.

The Online Book Initiative

The Online Book Initiative (OBI) was created to form a publicly accessible repository for the vast collections of books, conference proceedings, reference materials, etc., which can be freely shared.

Beyond machine-readable material, there are huge collections of printed material that could be redistributed if put online. They need people willing to organize informal projects to scan, type, or otherwise get the material into electronic form for inclusion in the Online Book Repository. Library and information scientists are sought to help create formats and structures for organizing the repository.

For further information about the OBI, contact

 Online Book Initiative
Software Tool & Die
1330 Beacon Street
Brookline, MA 02146
obi@world.std.com
(617) 739-0202

Two mailing lists, one for general discussion about OBI issues and another for announcements only, are maintained on world.std.com; write to 'obirequest@world.std.com' to join either list or both.

Project Gutenberg

The purpose of Project Gutenberg is to encourage the creation and distribution of English-language electronic texts. They assist in the selection of hardware and software as well as in their installation and use. Also, the project helps with scanning, spelling checkers, proofreading, etc. Their goal is to provide a collection of 10,000 of the most used books by the year 2001, and to reduce the effective costs to the user to a price of approximately one cent per book, plus the cost of media and shipping and handling. Thus, the entire cost of libraries of this nature will be approximately $100 plus incidental costs.

In the past, most of the electronic text work has been carried out by private, semi-private, or incorporated individuals, with several library or college collections being created, but being made up mostly of the works entered by individuals on their own time and expense. This labor has largely been either a labor of love, or a labor made by those who see future libraries as computer-searchable collections that can be transmitted via disks, phone lines, or other media at a fraction of the cost in money, time, and paper as present-day paper media. These electronic books will not have to be rebound, reprinted, reshelved, etc. They will not have to be reserved and restricted to use by one patron at a time. All materials will be available to all patrons from all locations at all times.

The use of this type of library will benefit librarians even more. The amount of information will be so much greater than that available in present-day libraries that people using the library will find it impossible to go it alone—assistance will be imperative for taking full advantage of what is available.

All interested parties are welcome to get involved with the creation and distribution of electronic texts, whether it's a commitment to typing, scanning, proofreading, collecting, or whatever your pleasure might be.

The system mrcnext.cso.uiuc.edu is home to the archives of Project Gutenberg; currently available etexts include *Peter Pan, Alice in Wonderland,* and *Paradise Lost.* Each piece added to the Gutenberg collection undergoes a thorough and complete copyright check, to ensure that it's legally redistributable.

For more information on Project Gutenberg, write to

 Project Gutenberg
Illinois Benedictine College
5700 College Road
Lisle, IL 60532-0900

or you can contact its Director, Michael Hart, at 'hart@vmd.cso.-uiuc.edu'. A listserv list ('GUTNBERG') is available for discussions about Project Gutenberg—send 'listserv@uiucvmd.bitnet' the command

sub gutnberg *Your Real Name*

The Usenet newsgroup bit.listserv.gutnberg is a gateway of the mailing list. See page 16 and Chapter 4, *Usenet News*, for more information on their respective areas.

Advances in Networking

 Research and development are two buzz words often heard when discussing the networking field—everything needs to go faster, over longer distances, for a lower cost. To "keep current," one should read the various trade magazines and newspapers, or frequent the networking-oriented newsgroups of Usenet. If possible, attend trade shows and symposia like Usenix, Interop, et al.

FrEdMail

The FrEdMail (Free Educational Mail) Network is an informal, grassroots telecommunications network that helps teachers and students exchange information freely and simply. With over 120 nodes, it lets teachers share experiences with student assignments, distribute teaching materials and curriculum ideas, and promote the development of effective reading and writing skills. FrEdMail also allows teachers to obtain information about workshops, job opportunities, and legislation affecting education. It motivates students to become better learners and writers. FrEdMail was initiated by Al Rogers, a computer specialist for San Diego County Schools.

The network has received nationwide recognition for its contributions to the pedagogy and practices of instructional telecommunications. In fact, the network has been so successful that it has influenced the development of commercial services such as the McGraw-Hill Information Exchange (MIX) and the AT&T Long Distance Learning Network.

FrEdMail consists of a number of electronic bulletin boards, each representing a "node" in the network. The bulletin boards are operated by individuals and institutions. While some are maintained at universities and others by district and county offices of education, many are operated at individual schools in actual school classrooms, offices, or even in teachers' homes. The idea of local ownership offers a number of advantages: each node is able to tailor content to its local needs, and some districts use the boards for instructional and administrative purposes. Other sites promote use by students at school or at home. The service is promoted locally by each site, and most are proactive in recruiting participants and training teachers.

In an effort to promote student and instructor participation in data telecommunications, CERFnet (the California Education and Research Federation Network) developed a prototype gateway between CERFnet and the FrEdMail Network. The gateway uses file-serving capabilities based on the Usenet model of conferences and selected news feeds, allowing a great deal of flexibility in linking FrEdMail users with other networks and educators on other systems all over the world. Fifteen selected FrEdMail sites will dial-up directly to their local CERFnet terminal server, which will act as the regional file server. In the prototype phase, out-of-state FrEdMail hubs would be linked directly to the server in San Diego via toll-free telephone calls.

CERFnet also wants to promote this prototype gateway to colleges and universities that want to serve their own local K-12 communities. Their vision is one of a national network of university academic computing labs that act as local file servers to their regional K-12 FrEdMail sites, using existing facilities and transportation networks.

For more information on FrEdMail, contact Al Rogers, executive director, by electronic mail at 'alrogers@cerf.net', or send a message to 'help@cerf.net'.

NREN

In December 1991, Congress passed the High Performance Computing and Communications (HPCC) Program. It will accelerate the development of a thousand-fold improvement in useful computing capability and a hundred fold improvement in available computer communications by 1996. It comprises four components: high-performance computing, development of new software technology and algorithms, better education and research support, and a gigabit network.

The fourth component, the National Research and Education Network (NREN), will have approximately 1000 times the present capacity of existing technology. It is for research and education, not general-purpose communication. Nonetheless, it will be fundamentally dependent upon its use as a testbed for new communications technologies. Enhanced image visualization and distributed computing will help with problems like medical diagnosis, aerodynamics, and global change. A collaborative effort between U.S. industry, the federal government, and the educational community should help usher in a new era in computing that will leave its mark in every facet of modern society.

A mailing list, 'nren-discuss@psi.com', is available for discussion of the NREN; write to 'nren-discuss-request@psi.com' to be added. For a booklet describing the HPCC, write to

Federal Coordinating Council
    for Science, Engineering and Technology
Committee on Physical, Mathematical, and
    Engineering Sciences
c/o National Science Foundation
Computer and Information Science and
    Engineering Directorate
1800 G Street, N.W.
Washington, D.C. 20550

Internet Talk Radio

The Internet now has its own global radio station, in the form of the Internet Talk Radio (ITR). Fashioned after similar conventional radio programs, ITR presents interviews and news stories about the Internet exclusively in electronic form.

Created by Carl Malamud, Internet Talk Radio has been

Courtesy of Carole Cable

"An earlier version of this novel appeared two years ago as a manicotti recipe on the Internet.

mentioned in "normal" press like *The Wall Street Journal* and *The New York Times*, and even discussed on its counterpart, National Public Radio. ITR is distributed as a set of (rather large) audio files which can be played on a variety of systems, including workstations from Sun Microsystems.

Regular features of ITR include "Geek of the Week," a traditional interview format with industry leaders and well-known net.citizens; the Incidental Tourist,[6] which offers restaurant reviews and travel tips for cities around the world; TechNation, a one-hour weekly radio show focusing on Americans and technology; and some occasional book reviews. New features are being developed for ITR on a regular basis—a close relationship with the National Press Club led to the first-ever Press Club luncheon broadcast on

6. The Incidental Tourist is a play on the title of Anne Tyler's fantastic book *The Accidental Tourist*, which I urge everyone to read.

the Internet. For many people, these luncheons are not very visible; they need to be either there, own a satellite dish, or subscribe to a cable provider who carries CSPAN. TechNation has featured such distinguished guests as Dr. Linus Pauling, two-time winner of the Nobel Prize, and Jane Metcalfe and Louis Rossetto, the editors and publishers of *Wired* magazine.

The ITR is based on the Internet multicast backbone (the *MBONE*). If you want to learn more about the MBONE, you can retrieve a frequently-asked questions list about it from `venera.isi.edu` in the directory '/mbone' as 'faq.txt'.

Each set of files in an ITR distribution is taped in the same professional environment that you would expect from typical radio—high-quality microphones, digital recorders, and top-of-the-line sound mixers. The files themselves are distributed around the Internet on a number of FTP sites. Write to 'info@radio.com' for the latest information. To find out how to play the files on your system, ask your system administrator or support staff for assistance.

Online Career Center

The Online Career Center database offers access to job listings and full-text resume files with online keyword searches to assist both employers and individuals in effectively using the Internet. Forty leading corporations in the United States have joined to create a non-profit organization to develop and manage the Career Center.

"To talk in publick, to think in solitude, to read and to hear, to inquire, and to answer inquiries, is the business of a scholar."

— Samuel Johnson,
Chapter VIII
The History of Rasselas, Prince of Abissinia

There are no charges for people to access the more than 8,000 job listings, view company information and profiles, enter resumes into the company-sponsored database, or email resumes to potential employers. You may also receive career assistance information on subjects like career fairs, job searches, resume writing, and other career resources.

To access the database, use gopher to connect to gopher.-msen.com. (See page 80 to learn how.) For more information on the Online Career Center, contact

William O. Warren
Executive Director
Online Career Center
3125 Dandy Trail
Indianapolis, IN 46214
occ@msen.com
(317) 293-6499

9 Finding Out More

Furthering your network education will be a challenge without some tips on where to look. In the realm of freely redistributable information, there are three main sources of information: the InterNIC Directory of Directories, a continuing attempt to catalogue the many resources available on the Net; MaasInfo, a well-composed set of files providing facts (and some strong opinions) about what's out there; and Requests for Comments, the Internet standards.

In the area of published work (aside from what you're holding), *The Matrix* by John Quarterman is invaluable if you want to know how the different networks are connected and who's responsible for what. An updated edition of O'Reilly and Associate's *Directory of Electronic Mail Addressing and Networks* offers information similar to that offered in *The Matrix*, but doesn't go into as much depth on how the networks fit together. Rather, it gives you information on how to contact the administrators of each network. To learn about computer networking in general, Andrew Tanenbaum's *Computer Networks* is an excellent text. Finally, to learn how the Internet protocols themselves operate, Douglas Comer wrote a series of books entitled *Internetworking With TCP/IP*, which discuss every aspect of the TCP/IP protocol suite.

Keep your eyes open—in the coming years, the information gap will be closing drastically. The technology is here, and people are willing to learn. The body of documentation will continue to grow by leaps and bounds.

Magazines and Newsletters

With the growing interest about the Internet in the publishing industry, a number of magazines are now entirely devoted to covering the Net, or have regular columns about it. In addition, according to Neal Stephenson in *The New Republic*, in June, July, and the first half of August of 1993, "major American newspapers carried 173 stories mentioning the Internet, compared with twenty-two a year earlier." This, combined with coverage in such truly mainstream publications as *Spin Magazine, The Atlantic*, and *Newsweek* are a strong indicator that the Net has begun to breech the barrier separating usage of the Internet from the public at large. A few of the available magazines and newsletters are mentioned here—keep an eye on the newsstands, though, since many more will be appearing in the future.

Internet World

Internet World, published by the Meckler Corporation, is a rich resource for Net surfers. Issues are monthly and cover a variety of topics, from new developments on the Internet (e.g., new services) to a spotlight on a particular service provider. Edited by Daniel Dern, each issue of *Internet World* proves to be well-written and interesting. It originally started out as a newsletter with distribution primarily among librarians and researchers; it has since been transformed into a mainstream glossy magazine with a very professional look. For subscription information, contact Meckler at

Meckler Corporation
11 Ferry Lane West
Westport, CT 06880
meckler@jvnc.net
(203) 226-6967
(203) 454-5840 (Fax)

Matrix News

Matrix Information and Directory Services, Inc., publishes a monthly newsletter called *Matrix News*. It discusses "the Matrix," the term for all of the computer networks worldwide that exchange electronic mail. Coverage includes Usenet, FidoNet, BITNET, the Internet, and conferencing systems like the Well and CompuServe. The newsletter is edited by John S. Quarterman (author of the very successful book *The Matrix*) and Smoot Carl-Mitchell.

What sets *Matrix News* apart from many other periodicals is its distribution method—you can either get copies in paper form, or you can receive it electronically. The publishers ask people not to redistribute copies they receive electronically, since it is not free and doing so would only make it more difficult to continue publishing the newsletter. They also publish through ClariNet (which is discussed in the next chapter), through the Usenet newsgroup clari.matrix_news.

You can also receive the *Matrix Maps Quarterly*; in addition to a regular subscription to *Matrix News*, you will receive full-color maps of the Internet's connectivity, size, growth, and other information.

Matrix News is very affordable, with rates comparable to those for other magazines and newsletters. To subscribe, write to

 Matrix Information and Directory Services, Inc.
1106 Clayton Lane, Suite 500W
Austin, TX 78723
mids@tic.com
(512) 451-7602
(512) 450-1436 (Fax)

Internet Columns

As the Internet makes its way into the corners of computing, more industry periodicals are recognizing that their readers are discovering the Net and need to know more about it. Among them are two magazines that previously catered mainly to people running private bulletin board systems (BBSs) and commercial online services.

The first, *Boardwatch Magazine*, includes articles about the Internet ranging from news and legal items that affect the Internet community to informational articles about how to use FTP, gopher, and other tools. Edited by Jack Rickard, *Boardwatch* is a must for any Net surfer's library.

Contact them at:

 Boardwatch Magazine
8500 West Bowles Ave., Suite 210
Littleton, CO 80123
subscriptions@boardwatch.com
(800) 933-6038 in the United States
(303) 973-6038 everywhere
(303) 973-3731 (Fax)

The second magazine of interest, *Online Access*, carries a column by Michael Strangelove covering many aspects of the Net. The bulk of its content is geared towards customers of major online services line CompuServe and Prodigy. Nonetheless, their regular Internet column and frequent features on special topics (e.g., the NREN and efforts to connect grade schools to the Net) are well worth the cost of an issue.

You can write to them for more information at

 Online Access Magazine
920 N. Franklin, Suite 203
Chicago, IL 60610-9588
Online_Access@portal.com

Note both *Boardwatch* and *Online Access* are probably available on your local newsstand or in a local bookstore, if you'd like to look at an issue before arranging for a subscription.

InterNIC Directory of Directories

 Until 1993, the NSF Network Service Center (NNSC) compiled the Internet Resource Guide (IRG). The goal of the guide was to increase the visibility of various Internet resources that may help users do their work better. While not an exhaustive list, the guide proved to be a useful compendium of many resources and a helpful reference for a new user.

During 1993, the Directory and Database Services area of the InterNIC began to merge the IRG into their own *InterNIC Directory of Direc-*

tories. The original information included in the IRG, ranging from library catalogs, network contact information, and supercomputer availability, will all be included in the new Directory. A new format, coupled with the latest information and new subject areas, will make the InterNIC directory a highly useful body of work. To find out about updates to the list, write admin@ds.internic.net.

The *Directory of Directories* is available via anonymous FTP from ds.internic.net in the directory '/resource'. It is split into various subdirectories based on subject area (e.g., 'archive', 'ftpsite', etc.). The original IRG is also available in the directory '/resource-guide.'

The NETA Diskette

The National Education and Technology Alliance (NETA), an educational non-profit organization, sells a diskette with information on getting an Internet connection, lists of providers with prices and reviews of their service, and other useful things. Contact them at

NETA
Box 6051
Lancaster, PA 17603
neta@holonet.net
(800) 457-9112 in the United States
(717) 898-9837 (Fax)

The MaasInfo Package

Robert E. Maas wrote a set of documents, collectively known as *MaasInfo*, that provide a good overview of how to use some of the services available over the Internet. He describes how to telnet directly to an NNTP port on a system if Usenet isn't available locally, how to use archie, and gives quick instructions on how to get started with BITNET listservs, how to use FTP, and other topics.

He also details information related to using networks. The most intriguing portion of his package is the "TopIndex"—a compilation of most of the known indexes to electronic information. It mentions things like the NICmaintained 'interest-groups' file, the nixpub Public Access Unix list, Billy Barron's list of online libraries, plus dozens of others. An excellent collection of network-oriented bibliographies is also included.

The package is available for anonymous FTP from aarnet.edu.au in the directory 'pub/doc'; each filename begins with the prefix "Maas".

John December s Internet CMC List

John December of the Rensselaer Polytechnic Institute maintains a list of information services concerning Internet computer-mediated communication (CMC). This useful guide is a gold mine; it includes pointers to files, services, and books about the Internet and CMC-related topics. Sections include The Internet and Services, Information Services and Electronic Publications, Societies and Organizations, and a Selected Bibliography. I urge everyone to get a copy of this document. It's on ftp.rpi.edu in the directory '/pub/communications/internet-cmc'.

Requests for Comments

The internal workings of the Internet are defined by a set of documents called RFCs (Request for Comments). The general process for creating an RFC is for someone wanting something formalized to write a document describing the issue and mail it to Jon Postel (postel@isi.edu). He acts as a referee for the proposal. It is then commented upon by all those wishing to take part in the discussion (electronically, of course). It may go through multiple revisions. Should it be generally accepted as a good idea, it will be assigned a number and filed with the RFCs.

There is a subset of RFCs called the FYIs (For Your Information documents). They are written in a language much more informal than that used in the other, standard RFCs. Topics range from answers to common questions for new and experienced users to a suggested bibliography.

Finally, as the Internet has grown and technology has changed, some RFCs have become unnecessary. These obsolete RFCs cannot be ignored, however. Frequently, when a change is made to some RFC that causes a new one to obsolete others, the new RFC only contains explanations and motivations for the change. Understanding the model on which the whole facility is based may involve reading the original and subsequent RFCs on the topic.

RFCs and FYIs are available via FTP from many sources, including:

- The ftp.internic.net archive, as '/rfc/rfcxxxx.txt', where *xxxx* is the number of the RFC.

- from ftp.uu.net, in the directory '/inet/rfc'.

- from ftp.nisc.sri.com, in '/rfc.'

They're also available via electronic mail by sending mail to the address mailserv@rs.internic.net with a 'Subject:' line of document-by-name rfc*xxxx* (again, *xxxx* is an RFC number). To learn about archive servers, consult Appendix B, *Retrieving Files via Email.*

"Knowledge is of two kinds. We know a subject ourselves, or we know where we can find information upon it."

— Samuel Johnson
Letter to Lord Chesterfield
February, 1755

Conclusion

The Internet changes on a daily (if not hourly) basis; this guide is simply a snapshot in time, certainly omitting some aspects of the Net. However, you should now have enough information to make the incredible breadth and complexity of the Internet a mite less imposing. Coupled with some exploration and experimentation, every user has the potential to be a competent net.citizen, using the facilities that are available to their fullest.

You, the reader, are *strongly* encouraged to suggest improvements to any part of this guide. If something was unclear, left you with doubts, or wasn't addressed, it should be fixed. Please report any problems or inaccuracies to 'guide-bugs@zen.org'.

If you are interested in discussion about information to be included or removed from this guide, write to 'guide-request@zen.org' to be placed on a mailing list for such things.

"I've seed de first an de last. . . : I seed de beginnin, en now I sees de endin. . . ."

— William Faulkner
The Sound & The Fury
April 8, 1928

125

A Getting to Other Networks

Interconnectivity has been and always will be one of the biggest goals in computer networking. The ultimate desire is to make it so one person can contact anyone else no matter where they are. A number of gateways between networks have been set up. They include:

ALANet	Members on the American Library Association Network can be reached as 'user%ALANET-@intermail.isi.edu'.
America Online	In 1992 America Online (AoL) brought live an email gateway to the Internet. To reach a user on AoL, address your mail as userid@aol.com'.
AppleLink	General Electric sells access to AppleLink, which is similar to QuantumLink for Commodore computers and PCLink for IBM

PCs and compatibles. It also provides email access through the address 'user@applelink.-apple.com'.

| ATTMail | AT&T sells a commercial email service called ATTMail. Its users can be reached by writing to 'user@attmail.com'. |

| BIX | Users on BIX (the Byte Information eXchange) can be reached at 'user@bix.com'. |

| CGNet | People with CGNet Services, a network of agricultural researchers, can be reached at 'user-%CGNET@intermail.ise.edu'. |

| CompuServe (CI$) | To reach a user on the commercial service CompuServe, you must address the mail as 'xxxxx.xxx-@compuserve.com', with xxxxx.xxx being their CompuServe user ID. Normally CompuServe ids are represented as |

being separated by a comma (like 71999,141); since most mailers don't react well to having commas in addresses, it was changed to a period. For the above address, mail would be sent to '71999.141–@compuserve.com'.

EcoNet

EcoNet is a community of persons using networks for information sharing and collaboration with respect to environmentally-oriented programs. Members of EcoNet can be reached with *'user-@igc.org'*.

FidoNet

The FidoNet computer network can be reached by using a special addressing method. If John Smith is on the node '1:2/3.4' on FidoNet, his or her email address would be 'john.smith@p**4**.f**3**.n**2**.z**1**.fido-net.org' (notice how each of the numbers falls in place?).

GEnie

General Electric Information Services runs GEnie, a commercial service offering many RoundTable discussions on a variety of topics, online air reservations, and other services. Contact users on GEnie by writing to '*user*@genie.-geis.com'. Note that GEnie users must pay an extra fee to receive mail from the Internet; if possible, verify that the person you're trying to reach has indeed paid the extra monthly charge.

GeoNet

Customers of the GeoNet mail service can be reached based upon which system they are on. For users in North America, write to '*user*:geo4@map.das.net'; in Europe, contact them as '*user*:geo1@map.das.net'; and finally, customers in the United Kingdom have an address resembling '*user*:geo2@map.-das.net'.

MCI Mail

MCI also sells email accounts (similar to ATTMail). Users can be reached by referring to their user ID number; it's guaranteed to be unique. Addresses take the form '*1234567*@mcimail.com'. If you're unsure about the numeric address, try sending mail to their last name instead of their ID number. If there's more than one person with that last name, MCImail will return your message with a list of users that match that name, along with their numeric addresses.

| **PeaceNet** | Users on the PeaceNet network can be reached by writing to '*user*@igc.org'. |

| **Prodigy** | The Prodigy online service boasts the most subscribers of any commercial service in the United States. As of late 1993, Internet access is still being set up for Prodigy users. Write to Prodigy users by addressing mail to '*userid*–@prodigy.com'. |

| **SCIENCEnet** | Operated by OMNet as part of SprintMail, SCIENCEnet offers email services for researchers in oceanography, astronomy, geology, and agriculture; it's also SCIENCEnet. Write to '[*user* /OMNET)MAIL/USA%–TELEMAIL@Intermail.ISI.edu'. |

The Well	Users on the online service The WELL can be reached by writing to 'user@well.sf.ca.us'. The Well is directly connected to the Internet.

WWIVnet	WWIVnet is a network of personal computers all running the WWIV BBS software. On WWIVnet, users are referred to as *user @node*. To reach them from the Internet, write to 'user node-@wwiv.tfsquad.mn.org'. Don't send large messages over this link, though—it is entirely composed of systems calling each others' modems, and the operators of those systems must pay for their phone calls out of their own pockets.

Note that some services are not (nor do they plan to be) accessible from the "outside" (like Prodigy); others, like GEnie and America Online, are actively investigating the possibility of creating a gateway into their system. For the latest information on mailing to various networks, consult a list called the *Inter-Network Mail Guide*. It's available from csd4.csd.uwm.edu in '/pub/internetwork-guide'. To find out if you can directly connect to a given commercial service through the Internet, your best chance for accurate information is to ask the service itself, through its customer service line.

B Retrieving Files via Email

For those who have a connection to the Internet but cannot FTP, there do exist a few alternatives to get those files you so desperately need. When requesting files, it's imperative that you keep in mind the size of your request—odds are the other people who may be using your link won't be too receptive to sudden bursts of really heavy traffic on their normally sedate connection.

Archive Servers

An alternative to the currently well-over used FTPmail system is taking advantage of the many *archive servers* that are presently being maintained. These are programs that receive email messages which contain commands, and act on them. For example, sending an archive server the command 'help' will usually yield, in the form of a piece of email, information on how to use the various commands that the server has available.

One such archive server is 'mailserv.internic.net'. Maintained by the Resource Services part of the InterNIC, the server is set up to make all of the information at the NIC available for people who don't have access to FTP. This also includes the WHOIS service (see page 84). Some sample 'Subject:' lines for queries to the InterNIC server are:

Subject: help	*Describes available commands.*
Subject: document-by-name rfc822	*Sends a copy of RFC-822.*

133

Subject: document-by-name rfc-index	*Sends an index of the available RFCs.*
Subject: netinfo domain-template.txt	*Sends a domain application.*
Subject: whois mit	*Sends WHOIS information on 'mit'.*

More information on using their archive server can be obtained by writing to their server address service@nic.ddn.mil with a 'Subject:' of help.

There are different "brands" of archive server, each with its own set of commands and services. Among them there often exists a common set of commands and services (e.g., 'index', 'help', etc.). Be that as it may, one should always consult the individual help for a specific server before assuming the syntax—100K surprises can be hard on a system.

FTP-by-Mail Servers

 Some systems offer people the ability to receive files through a mock FTP interface via email. See Chapter 3, *Anonymous FTP,* for a general overview of how to FTP. The effects of providing such a service vary, although a rule of thumb is that it will probably use a substantial amount of the available resources on a system.

The "original" FTP-by-Mail service, BITFTP, is available to BITNET users from the Princeton node PUCC. It was once accessible to anyone, but had to be closed out to non-BITNET users because of the heavy load on the system.

In part because of this closure, Paul Vixie announced the existence of a system called FTPmail, available through one of Digital's gateway computers, decwrl.dec.com. Write to 'ftpmail@decwrl.dec.com' with 'help' in the body of the letter for instructions on its use. For European users, send mail to 'ftpmail@grasp.insa-lyon.fr'.

C Newsgroup Creation

Everyone has the opportunity to make a *Call For Votes* on the Usenet and attempt to create a newsgroup that he feels would be of benefit to the general readership. The rules governing newsgroup creation have evolved over the years into a generally accepted method. They only govern the "world" groups; they aren't applicable to regional or other alternative hierarchies.

Discussion

A discussion must first take place to address issues like the naming of the group, where in the group tree it should go (e.g., rec.sports.koosh vs. rec.games.koosh?), and whether or not it should be created in the first place. The formal *Request For Discussion* (RFD) should be posted to news.announce.newgroups, along with any other groups or mailing lists at all related to the proposed topic. news.announce.newgroups is moderated. You should place it first in the 'Newsgroups:' header, so that it will get mailed to the moderator only. The article won't immediately be posted to the other newsgroups listed; rather, it will give you the opportunity to have the moderator correct any inconsistencies or mistakes in your RFD. He will take care of posting it to the newsgroups you indicated. Also the 'Followup-To:' header will be set so that the actual discussion takes place only in news.groups. If a user has difficulty posting to a moderated group, a submission intended for news.announce.newgroups can be mailed to the address 'announce-newgroups@rpi.edu'.

The final name and *charter* of the group, and whether it will be moderated or unmoderated, will be determined during the discussion period. If it's to be moderated, the discussion will also decide who the moderator will be. If there's no general agreement on these points among those in favor of a new group at the end of 30 days, the discussion will be taken into mail rather than continue being posted to news.groups; that way, the proponents of the group can iron out their differences and come back with a proper proposal, and make a new Request For Discussion.

Voting

 After the discussion period (which is mandatory), if it's been determined that a new group really is desired, a name and charter are agreed upon, and it's been determined whether the group will be moderated (and by whom), a *Call For Votes* (CFV) should be posted to news.announce.newgroups, along with any other groups that the original Request For Discussion was posted to. The CFV should be posted (or mailed to the news.announce.-newgroups moderator) as soon as possible after the discussion ends (to keep it fresh in everyone's mind).

The Call for Votes should include clear instructions on how to cast a vote. It's important that it be clearly explained how to both vote for *and* against a group (and be of equivalent difficulty or ease). If it's easier for you or your administrator, two separate addresses can be used for yes and no votes, providing that they're on the same machine. Regardless of the method, everyone must have a very specific idea of how to get his/her vote counted.

The voting period can last between 21 and 31 days, no matter what the preliminary results of the vote are. A vote can't be called off simply because 400 "no" votes have come in and only two "yes" votes. The Call for Votes should include the exact date that the voting period will end—only those votes arriving on the vote-taker's machine before this date can be counted.

To keep awareness high, the CFV can be repeated during the vote, provided that it gives the same clear, unbiased instructions for casting a vote as the original; it also has to be the same proposal as was first posted. The charter can't change mid-vote. Also, votes that are posted don't count—only those that were mailed to the vote-taker can be tallied.

Partial results should *never* be included; only a statement of the specific proposal, that a vote is in progress on it, and how to cast a vote. A mass acknowledgment ("Mass ACK" or "Vote ACK") is permitted; however, it must be presented in a way that gives no indication of which way a person voted. One way to avoid this is to create one large list of *everyone* who's voted, and sort it in alphabetical order. It should not be two sorted lists (of the yes and no votes, respectively).

Every vote is autonomous. The votes for or against one group can't be transferred to another, similar proposal. A vote can only count for the *exact* proposal to which it was a response. In particular, a vote for or against a newsgroup under one name can't be counted as a vote for or against another group with a different name or charter, a different moderated/unmoderated status, or, if it's moderated, a different moderator or set of moderators. Whew!

Finally, the vote has to be explicit; they should be of the form 'I vote for the group foo.bar as proposed' or 'I vote against the group foo.bar as proposed'. The wording doesn't have to be exact, your intention just has to be clear.

The Result of a Vote

At the end of the voting period, the vote-taker has to post (to news.announce.newgroups) the tally and email addresses of the votes received. Again, it can also be posted to any of the groups listed in the original CFV. The tally should make clear which way a person voted, so the results can be verified if it proves necessary to do so.

After the vote result is posted to news.announce.newgroups, there is a mandatory five-day waiting period. This affords everyone the opportunity to correct any errors or inconsistencies in the voter list or the voting procedure.

Creation of the Group

 If, after the waiting period, there are no serious objections that might invalidate the vote, the vote is put to the "water test." If there were 100 more valid 'YES/create' votes than 'NO/don't create' votes, *and* at least two-thirds of the total number of votes are in favor of creation, then a new-group control message can be sent out (often by the moderator of news.announce.-newgroups). If the 100-vote margin or the two-thirds percentage isn't met, the group has failed and can't be created.

If the proposal failed, all is not lost—after a six-month waiting period (a "cooling down"), a new Request For Discussion can be posted to news.groups, and the whole process can start over again. If after a couple of tries it becomes obvious that the group is *not* wanted or needed, the votetaker should humbly step back and accept the opinion of the majority. (As life goes, so goes Usenet.)

D Items Available for FTP

What follows is a listing of the FTPable items that are mentioned in this book; they are listed in the order of their appearance. For more information on actually retrieving them, read Chapter 3, *Anonymous FTP.*

Interest Groups

ftp.internic.net */netinfo*	The file interest-groups is a full listing of nearly every known mailing list.

Listserv

cs.bu.edu */pub/listserv*	An implementation of the listserv system for Unix is available; it emulates much of the functionality of its BITNET counterpart.

FAQs

rtfm.mit.edu */pub/usenet*	The RTFM archives include the Frequently Asked Questions lists

for nearly every Usenet news-group. The filenames are simply their 'Subject:' headers with underscores in place of spaces. There are also truncated file-names, in case your system can't handle really long names.

St. George

nic.cerf.net
/cerfnet/cerfnet_info
/library_catalog

The file internet-catalogs has a date suffix indicating the most recent version of the St. George Directory. It also includes infor-mation on Internet BBSs and other things.

Library List

ftp.unt.edu
/pub/library

Billy Barron's list of access information for a substantial number of the libraries that are accessible over the Internet. The file 'libraries.txt' is a plain ASCII version; Postscript and WordPerfect 5 versions are also available.

Internet Services List

csd4.csd.uwm.edu /pub	Scott Yanoff's list of Internet services is stored in the file 'inet.services.txt'; it's also posted regularly to the Usenet newsgroups alt.bbs.internet and alt.internet.services.

Hytelnet

access.usask.ca /pub/hytelnet	Versions of the hytelnet program are available for IBM PCs, Unix-based systems, and Vaxen running VMS. To work on your PC, you must have the appropriate software and hardware needed to do a telnet.

NIST Guide

csrc.ncsl.nist.gov /pub/nistir	A guide to using the NIST computer security BBS is available as the file 'bbsguide.txt'.

WAIS Software

ftp.cnidr.org /wais	Software and documentation for the Wide Area Information Servers.

WHOIS List

sipb.mit.edu /pub/whois	Matt Power's list of sites offering WHOIS services is stored in the file 'whois-servers.list'.

Clarinet

ftp.uu.net /Clarinet	This directory houses information on the Clarinet news service.

EFF

ftp.eff.org /pub/EFF	Information on the Electronic Frontier Foundation, including back issues of *EFFector Online* and *EFFnews* is available, along with the EFF mission statement and related documents.

GNU

prep.ai.mit.edu /pub/gnu	The software produced by the GNU Project is freely redistributable; the amount and variety are growing by leaps and bounds.

LPF

prep.ai.mit.edu */pub/lpf*	The League for Programming Freedom has a large body of information related to patents and intellectual property.

Project Gutenberg

mrcnext.cso.uiuc.edu */etext*	Project Gutenberg offers the freed texts of books like *Peter Pan* and *Alice in Wonderland.*

MBONE

venera.isi.edu */mbone*	The frequently asked questions list for the Internet multicast backbone (the "MBONE") is available in the file 'faq.txt'.

Directory of Directories

ds.internic.net */resource*	The InterNIC *Directory of Directories* is divided into various subject areas. It includes the information that was contained in the now-defunct Internet Resource Guide.

MaasInfo

aarnet.edu.au */pub/doc*	The MaasInfo documents include information on using basic Internet services, as well as an "index of indexes".

RFCs

ftp.internic.net */rfc*	The Internet Requests for Comments are available on the NIC; some of them, including the FYI series, will be of interest to new users. The files 'fyi-index.-txt' and 'rfc-index.txt' list the topics of each FYI/RFC, and 'std-index.txt' lists the title of each RFC that is also an Internet standard.

Internet CMC

ftp.rpi.edu */pub/communications* */internet-cmc*	John December's fantastic list of information sources about the Internet and computer-mediated communication.

Internet Mailing Guide

ra.msstate.edu */pub/docs*	The Guide provides the nitty-gritty for going "from here to there"—it is updated semi-regularly.

NixPub

gvl.unisys.com
/pub/nixpub

The NixPub list provides information on Public Access Unix
systems around the world.

Jargon File

prep.ai.mit.edu
/pub/gnu

The Jargon File, an online compendium of network lore, is in
the file 'jargon*nnn*.ascii.Z',
with *nnn* being the latest version.
The New Hacker's Dictionary is
based upon this file.

E | Services via Telnet

When the second edition of *Zen* came out, one of the most common requests I had was to include an appendix, similar to the previous one, listing all of the telnetable services named in the book. I encourage you to get a copy of Scott Yanoff's list of Internet services (see page 60 for the details) for the latest information on what you can access over the Net.

AIP

pinet.aip.org *new*	Log in as new with a password of new to use the Physics Information Network at the American Institute of Physics. You will need to register.

APA

eis.calstate.edu *bbs*	A BBS run by the American Philosophical Association.

Air Pollution

ttnbbs.rtpnc.epa.gov *none*	A BBS run by the United States Environmental Protection Agency.

Archie

archie.sura.net *archie*	Log in as *archie* to use the Archie database.

BIX

bix.com *account*	The BIX commercial online service.

CARL

pac.carl.org *none*	You don't need a login ID to use CARL; offers library databases, book reviews, and other useful databases.

Clemson Forestry and Agriculture

eureka.clemson.edu *PUBLIC*	Information about forestry and agriculture, mainly of the Southeastern United States.

CompuServe

hermes.merit.edu *compuserve*	The CompuServe commercial online service.

Dante Project

library.dartmouth.edu *connect dante*	The Dartmouth College Dante Project.

Denver University

nyx.cs.du.edu *new*	The NYX BBS in Colorado.

E-Math

e-math.ams.com *e-math*	The American Mathematical Society (AMS).

FDA

fdabbs.fda.gov *bbs*	The United States Food and Drug Administration.

FEDIX

fedix.fie.com *fedix*	Information on scholarships, fellowships, minority colleges and universities, etc.

Freenet

freenet-in-a.cwru.edu *none*	You don't need a login ID initially when connecting to the Cleveland Freenet; rather, it will walk you through a registration process.

GEnie

hermes.merit.edu *sprintnet-313171*	The GEnie commercial online service.

Geographic Server

geoserver.eecs. **umich.edu** *port 3000*	Find out information by city, zip code, etc.

Gopher

consultant.micro. **umn.edu** *gopher*	An account that will let you try the Internet gopher.

HP Calculators

hpcvbbs.cv.hp.com *new*	A BBS for fans of Hewlett-Packard advanced calculators.

HYTELNET

access.usask.ca *hytelnet*	The HYTELNET service helps you navigate your way around a selection of libraries and other telnetable services.

Ham Radio Callbook

callsign.cs.buffalo.edu *port 2000*	Information on ham radio call-signs, searchable by different criteria.

JewishNet

vms.huji.ac.il *jewishnet*	A BBS for members of the Jewish religion.

Knowbot

nri.reston.va.us *port 185*	Lets you search the White Pages directory.

LawNet

lawnet.law. columbia.edu *lawnet*	Online law library, info on law firms, the U.S. courts, and a gateway into HYTELNET.

Library of Congress

locis.loc.gov *none*	You don't need an ID to search the catalogs, copyright information, federal legislation, and other items at the Library of Congress.

NASA Extragalactic Database

ned.ipac.caltech.edu *ned*	The NASA/IPAC database on extragalactic objects.

NASA SpaceLink

spacelink.msfc. nasa.gov *NEWUSER*	Space-related information, including NASA news.

NICOL

nicol.jvnc.net *nicol*	Information on JVNCnet, its members, and other Internet activities. Also access to the Meckler MC(2) electronic information service.

NIST Computer Security

cs-bbs.ncsl.nist.gov *none*	You don't need a login ID (you will need to register, though) to use the computer-security BBS run by the National Institute of Standards and Technology.

Net Mail Sites

hermes.merit.edu *netmailsites*	Search for a given university, company, or other network party to find out their email address.

Netfind

bruno.cs.colorado.edu *netfind*	A netfind server; also try `netfind.oc.com`.

Newton

newton.dep.anl.gov *cocotext*	A BBS for people teaching or studying science, math, or computer science. NOT related to the Newton handheld computer.

OCEANIC

delocn.udel.edu *INFO*	An interactive database of research information covering all aspects of marine studies.

PENpages

psupen.psu.edu *PNOTPA*	Database of agricultural information.

PSI White Pages

wp.psi.net *fred*	PSI also maintains a directory of information in White Pages format.

Rutgers University

quartz.rutgers.edu *bbs*	A popular BBS run by Rutgers.

STIS

stis.nsf.gov *public*	National Science Foundation publications, grant request forms, etc.

SuperNet

supernet.ans.net *supernet*	News, information on the Internet, a Job Bank, and supercomputing magazines and related issues.

University of Iowa

bbs.isca.uiowa.edu *guest*	The ISCA bulletin-board system.

UMD Info Database

info.umd.edu *info*	Tons of distributed information.

UNC Chapel Hill

launchpad.unc.edu *launch*	A BBS run by the folks at the University of North Carolina.

WAIS

quake.think.com *wais*	An account that will let you do WAIS searches.

Washington University

wugate.wustl.edu *services*	A gateway into a huge array of online services available over the Internet.

Weather Service

downwind.sprl. umich.edu *port 3000*	A database of weather and related information, including current weather and forecasts; located at the University of Michigan.

Weather Service

wind.atmos.uah.edu *port 3000*	Another weather server, from the University of Alabama at Huntsville.

White House

sunsite.unc.edu *gopher*	A gopher interface to the main repository of information on the White House and the United States government.

F Country Codes

This appendix lists the known country codes as defined in the ISO-3166 standard.

af	Afghanistan	am	Armenia
al	Albania	aw	Aruba
dz	Algeria	au	Australia
as	American Samoa	at	Austria
ad	Andorra	az	Azerbaijan
ao	Angola	bs	Bahamas
aq	Antarctica	bh	Bahrain
ag	Antigua	bd	Bangladesh
ar	Argentina	bb	Barbados

by	Belarus	bn	Brunei
be	Belgium	bg	Bulgaria
bz	Belize	bf	Burkina Faso
bj	Benin	bi	Burundi
bm	Bermuda	kh	Cambodia
bt	Bhutan	cm	Cameroon
bo	Bolivia	ca	Canada
ba	Bosnia-Hercegovina	ct	Canton and Enderbury Islands
bw	Botswana	cv	Cape Verde
bv	Bouvet Island	ky	Cayman Islands
br	Brazil	cf	Central Africa Republic
io	British Indian Ocean Territory	td	Chad

cl	Chile	cz	Czech Republic
cn	China	dk	Denmark
cx	Christmas Island	dj	Djibouti
cc	Cocos (Keeling) Islands	dm	Dominica
co	Columbia	do	Dominican Republic
km	Comoros	tp	East Timor
cg	Congo	ec	Ecuador
ck	Cook Islands	eg	Egypt
cr	Costa Rica	sv	El Salvador
ci	Cote d'Ivoire	gq	Equatorial Guinea
hr	Croatia	ee	Estonia
cu	Cuba	et	Ethiopia
cy	Cyprus	fk	Falkland Islands

fo	Faroe Islands	**gr**	Greece
fj	Fiji	**gl**	Greenland
fi	Finland	**gd**	Grenada
fr	France	**gp**	Guadeloupe
gf	French Guiana	**gu**	Guam
pf	French Polynesia	**gt**	Guatemala
tf	French Southern Territories	**gn**	Guinea
ga	Gabon	**gw**	Guinea-Bisseu
gm	Gambia	**gy**	Guyana
ge	Georgia	**ht**	Haiti
de	Germany	**hm**	Heard and McDonald Islands
gh	Ghana	**hn**	Honduras
gi	Gibraltar	**hk**	Hong Kong

hu	Hungary	kz	Kazakhstan
is	Iceland	ke	Kenya
in	India	ki	Kiribati
id	Indonesia	kp	Demo. People's Rep. of Korea
ir	Iran	kr	Republic of Korea
iq	Iraq	kw	Kuwait
ie	Ireland	kg	Kyrgystan
il	Israel	la	Lao People's Demo. Republic
it	Italy	lb	Lebanon
jm	Jamaica	ls	Lesotho
jp	Japan	lr	Liberia
jo	Jordan	ly	Libyan Arab Jamahiriya

li	Liechtenstein	mx	Mexico
lt	Lithuania	fm	Micronesia
lu	Luxembourg	md	Moldova
mo	Macau	mc	Monaco
mg	Madagascar	mn	Mongolia
mw	Malawi	ms	Montserrat
my	Malaysia	ma	Morocco
mv	Maldives	mz	Mozambique
ml	Mali	mm	Myanmar
mt	Malta	na	Namibia
mh	Marshall Islands	nr	Nauru
mq	Martinique	np	Nepal
mr	Mauritania	nl	Netherlands
mu	Mauritius	an	Netherlands Antilles

nt	Neutral Zone	pa	Panama
nc	New Caledonia	pg	Papua New Guinea
nz	New Zealand	py	Paraguay
ni	Nicaragua	pe	Peru
ne	Niger	ph	Phillipines
ng	Nigeria	pn	Pitcairn Island
nu	Niue	pl	Poland
nf	Norfolk Island	pt	Portugal
mp	Northern Mariana Islands	pr	Puerto Rico
no	Norway	qa	Qatar
om	Oman	re	Re'union
pk	Pakistan	ro	Romania
pw	Palau	ru	Russian Federation

rw	Rwanda	sl	Sierra Leone
sh	St. Helena	sg	Singapore
kn	St. Kitts Nevis Anguilla	sk	Slovakia
lc	Saint Lucia	si	Slovenia
pm	St. Pierre and Miquelon	sb	Solomon Islands
vc	St. Vincent and the Grenadines	so	Somalia
ws	Samoa	za	South Africa
sm	San Marino	es	Spain
st	Sao Tome and Principe	lk	Sri Lanka
sa	Saudi Arabia	sd	Sudan
sn	Senegal	sr	Suriname
sc	Seychelles	sj	Svalbard and Jan Mayen Islands

sz	Swaziland	tr	Turkey
se	Sweden	tm	Turkmenistan
ch	Switzerland	tc	Turks and Caicos Islands
sy	Syria	tv	Tuvalu
tw	Taiwan	ug	Uganda
tj	Tajikistan	ua	Ukraine
tz	Tanzania	ae	United Arab Emirates
th	Thailand	gb	United Kingdom
tg	Togo	us	United States
tk	Tokelau	pu	U.S. Misc. Pacific Islands
to	Tonga	uy	Uruguay
tt	Trinidad and Tobago	uz	Uzbekistan
tn	Tunisia	vu	Vanuatu

va	Vatican City State	eh	Western Sahara
ve	Venezuela	ye	Yemen
vn	Vietnam	yu	Yugoslavia
vg	Virgin Islands (British)	zr	Zaire
vi	Virgin Islands (U.S.)	zm	Zambia
wf	Wallis and Futuma Islands	zw	Zimbabwe

Glossary

This glossary is only a tiny subset of all of the various terms and other things that people regularly use on the Net. For a more complete (and very entertaining) reference, it's suggested you get a copy of *The New Hacker's Dictionary*, which is based on a very large text file called the Jargon File. Edited by Eric Raymond (eric@snark.thyrsus.com), the dictionary is available from the MIT Press, Cambridge, Massachusetts, 02142; its ISBN number is 0-262-68069-6. For FTP information on the Jargon File, consult Appendix D, *Items Available for FTP.* Definitions in this glossary that are in any way derived from the Jargon File or the *New Hacker's Dictionary* are marked with "(NHD)." Also see RFC-1392, the *Internet Users' Glossary,* for a less entertaining but highly useful glossary.

:-) This odd symbol is one of the ways a person can portray "mood" in the very flat medium of computers—by using "smilies." This is "meta-communication," and there are literally hundreds of them, from the obvious to the obscure. This particular example expresses "happiness." Don't see it? Tilt your head to the left 90 degrees. Smilies are also used to denote sarcasm. There are actually a few small booklets on smilies available in many bookstores.

address resolution   Conversion of an Internet address to the corresponding physical address. On an ethernet, resolution requires broadcasting on the local area network.

administrivia   Administrative tasks, most often related to the maintenance of mailing lists, digests, news gateways, etc.

anonymous FTP   Also known as "anon FTP"; a service provided to make files available to the general Internet community—see Chapter 3, *Anonymous FTP.*

ANSI   The American National Standards Institute disseminates basic standards like ASCII, and acts as the United States' delegate to the ISO. Standards can be ordered from ANSI by writing to the ANSI Sales Department, 1430 Broadway, New York, NY 10018.

archie   A service that provides lookups for packages in a database of the offerings of countless of anonymous FTP sites. For a full description of archie and its offerings, see page 29.

archive server   An email-based file transfer facility offered by some systems.

ARPA (Advanced Research Projects Agency)   Former name of DARPA (Defense Advanced Research Projects Agency), the government agency that funded ARPAnet and later the DARPA Internet.

ARPAnet   A pioneering long-haul network funded by ARPA. It served as the basis for early networking research as well as a central backbone during the development of the Internet. The ARPAnet consisted of individual packet switching computers interconnected by leased lines. The ARPAnet no longer exists as a singular entity.

asynchronous   Transmission by individual bytes, not related to specific timing on the transmitting end.

auto-magic Something which happens pseudo-automatically, and is usually too complex to go into any further than to say it happens "automagically."

backbone A high-speed connection within a network that connects shorter, usually slower circuits. Also used in reference to a system that acts as a "hub" for activity (although those are becoming much less prevalent now than they were ten years ago).

bandwidth The capacity of a medium to transmit a signal. More informally, the mythical "size" of the Net, and its ability to carry the files and messages of those that use it. Some view certain kinds of traffic (FTPing hundreds of graphics images, for example) as a "waste of bandwidth" and look down upon them.

BITNET (Because It's Time Network) An NJE-based international educational network.

bounce The return of a piece of mail because of an error in its delivery.

btw An abbreviation for "by the way."

CFV (Call For Votes) Initiates the voting period for a Usenet newsgroup. At least one (occasionally two or more) email address is customarily included as a repository for the votes. See Appendix C, *Newsgroup Creation,* for a full description of the Usenet voting process.

ClariNews   The fee-based Usenet newsfeed available from Clari-Net Communications.

client   The user of a network service; also used to describe a computer that relies upon another for some or all of its resources.

CMC   Computer-mediated communication.

Cyberspace   A term coined by William Gibson in his fantasy novel *Neuromancer* to describe the "world" of computers and the society that gathers around them.

datagram   The basic unit of information passed across the Internet. It contains a source and destination address along with data. Large messages are broken down into a sequence of IP datagrams.

disassembling   Converting a binary program into human-readable machine language code.

DNS (Domain Name System)   The method used to convert Internet names to their corresponding Internet numbers.

domain   A part of the naming hierarchy. Syntactically, a domain name consists of a sequence of names or other words separated by dots.

dotted quad   A set of four numbers connected with periods that make up an Internet address; for example, 147.31.254.130.

email   The vernacular abbreviation for electronic mail.

email address   The UUCP or domain-based address by which a user is referred to. For example, Janis Joplin's UUCP address might be 'benz!janis,' while 'janis@porsche.-friend.org' could be her domain-based address.

Ethernet   A 10-million bit-per-second networking scheme originally developed by Xerox Corporation. Ethernet is widely used for LANs because it can network a wide variety of computers, it is not proprietary, and components are widely available from many commercial sources.

FDDI (Fiber Distributed Data Interface)   An emerging standard for network technology based on fiber optics that has been established by ANSI. FDDI specifies a 100-million bit-per-second data rate. The access control mechanism uses token-ring technology.

flame   Mail or a Usenet posting which is violently argumentative.

flamefest   Massive flaming.

foo   A place-holder for nearly anything—a variable, function, procedure, or even person. "A given user *foo* has the address 'foo@bar.com'." The NHD has an excellent (one entire page) definition and historical background for foo.

FQDN (Fully Qualified Domain Name)   The FQDN is the full site name of a system, rather than just its hostname. For example, the system lisa at Widener University has a FQDN of lisa.cs.widener.edu.

FTP (File Transfer Protocol)   The Internet standard high-level protocol for transferring files from one computer to another.

FYI   An abbreviation for the phrase "for your information." There is also a series of RFCs put out by the Network Information Center called FYIs; they address common questions of new users and many other useful things. See page 122 for instructions on retrieving FYIs.

gateway A special-purpose dedicated computer that attaches to two or more networks and routes packets from one network to the other. In particular, an Internet gateway routes IP datagrams among the networks it connects. Gateways route packets to other gateways until they can be delivered to the final destination directly across one physical network.

GopherSpace   The vast number of servers and areas of interest accessible through the Internet gopher.

GUI (Graphical User Interface)   The aspects of a windowing system that make it unique; for example, the Motif GUI has a 3D feel to its buttons and menus.

header   The portion of a packet, preceding the actual data, containing source and destination addresses and error-checking fields. Also part of a message or news article.

hits   Matches found in a search; e.g., a Veronica search for "NASA" will return a long list of hits for your query.

hostname   The name given to a machine. (See also **FQDN**.)

IMHO (In My Humble Opinion)   This usually accompanies a statement that may bring about personal offense or strong disagreement.

internet A collection of computers linked together by one or more networking protocols. An "internet" is not the same as "the Internet."

Internet A concatenation of many individual TCP/IP campus, state, regional, and national networks (such as NSFnet, AARNet, and Milnet) into one single logical network all sharing a common addressing scheme.

Internet number The dotted-quad address used to specify a certain system. The Internet number for cs.widener.edu is 147.31.254.130. A resolver is used to translate between hostnames and Internet addresses.

interoperate The ability of multivendor computers to work together using a common set of protocols. With interoperability, PCs, Macs, Suns, Dec VAXen, CDC Cybers, etc. all work together allowing one host computer to communicate with and take advantage of the resources of another.

ISO (International Organization for Standardization) Coordinator of the main networking standards that are put into use today.

kernel The level of an operating system or networking system that contains the system-level commands or all of the functions hidden from the user. In a Unix system, the kernel is a program that contains the device drivers, the memory management routines, the scheduler, and system calls. This program is always running while the system is operating.

LAN (Local Area Network) Any physical network technology that operates at high speed over short distances (up to a few thousand meters).

mail gateway   A machine that connects to two or more electronic mail systems (especially dissimilar mail systems on two different networks) and transfers mail messages among them.

mailing list   A possibly moderated discussion group, distributed via email from a central computer maintaining the list of people involved in the discussion.

mail path   A series of machine names used to direct electronic mail from one user to another.

MBONE   The Internet multicast backbone (the MBONE) is a "virtual network" which provides for Internet multicast packets to be routed across the Internet to a number of sites.

medium   The material used to support the transmission of data. This can be copper wire, coaxial cable, optical fiber, or electromagnetic wave (as in microwave).

multicast   A multicast packet is one which is intended to be received by a number of hosts.

multiplex   The division of a single transmission medium into multiple logical channels supporting many simultaneous sessions. For example, one network may have simultaneous FTP, telnet, rlogin, and SMTP connections, all going at the same time.

net.citizen   An inhabitant of Cyberspace. One usually tries to be a good net.citizen, lest one be flamed.

netiquette   A pun on "etiquette"; proper behavior on the Net. See page 46.

network   A group of machines connected together so they can transmit information to one another. There are two kinds of networks: local networks and remote networks.

NFS (Network File System)   A method developed by Sun Microsystems to allow computers to share files across a network in a way that makes them appear as if they're "local" to the system.

NIC   The DDN Network Information Center.

nixpub   A list maintained by Phil Eschallier (phil@ls.com) since 1987 detailing information on public access Unix systems. Two versions, a long one providing all information and a short one listing the vital statistics of each site, are available on gvl.unisys.com in 'pub/nixpub'. It's also regularly posted to the comp.misc newsgroup.

NNTP (Network News Transfer Protocol)   The standard for Internet exchange of Usenet messages, published in RFC-977, *Network News Transfer Protocol: A Proposed Standard for the Stream-Based Transmission of News.*

node   A computer that is attached to a network; also called a host.

NSFnet   The national backbone network, funded by the National Science Foundation and operated by the Merit Corporation, used to interconnect regional (mid-level) networks such as WestNet to one another.

NTP   The Network Time Protocol was developed to maintain a common sense of "time" among Internet hosts around the world. Many systems on the Internet run NTP, and have the same time (relative to Greenwich Mean Time), with a maximum difference of about one second.

packet   The unit of data sent across a packet switching network. The term is used loosely. While some Internet literature uses it to refer specifically to data sent across a physical network, other literature views the Internet as a packet-switching network and describes IP datagrams as packets.

pass line   A bet placed in the *pass line* of a craps table wins on the first roll of the dice yielding a 7 or 11 (termed a "natural"), and loses if a 2, 3, or 12 comes up (called a "craps"). If none of these numbers appear, the value thrown becomes the "point," which must be rolled again before a 7 in order to win.

polling   Connecting to another system to check for things like mail or news.

postmaster   The person responsible for taking care of mail problems, answering queries about users, and performing similar work for a given site.

protocols   A formal description of message formats and the rules two computers must follow to exchange those messages. Protocols can describe low-level details of machine-to-machine interfaces (e.g., the order in which bits and bytes are sent across a wire) or high-level exchanges between allocation programs (e.g., the way in which two programs transfer a file across the Internet).

recursion   The facility of a programming language to be able to call functions from within themselves.

resolve   Translate an Internet name into its equivalent IP address or other DNS information.

RFD (Request For Discussion)   Usually a two- to three-week period in which the particulars of newsgroup creation are battled out.

route   The path that network traffic takes from its source to its destination.

router   A dedicated computer (or other device) that sends packets from one place to another, paying attention to the current state of the network.

RTFM (Read The Fantastic Manual)   This acronym is often used when someone asks a simple or common question. The word "Fantastic" is usually replaced with one much more vulgar.

server   A computer that shares its resources, such as printers and files, with other computers on the network. An example of this is a Network File System (NFS) server, which shares its disk space with other computers.

signal-to-noise ratio   When used in reference to Usenet activity, "signal-to-noise ratio" describes the relation between the amount of actual information in a discussion compared to quantity. More often than not, there's substantial activity in a newsgroup, but a very small number of those articles actually contain anything useful.

signature   The small, usually four-line message at the bottom of a piece of email or Usenet article. In Unix, it's added by creating a file '.signature' in the user's home directory. Large signatures are a no-no.

smilies   See :-), page 167 .

SMTP (Simple Mail Transfer Protocol)   The Internet standard protocol for transferring electronic mail messages from one computer to another. SMTP specifies how two mail systems interact and the format of control messages they exchange to transfer mail.

summarize   To encapsulate a number of responses into one coherent, usable message. Often done on controlled mailing lists or active newsgroups to help reduce bandwidth.

synchronous   Data communications in which transmissions are sent at a fixed rate, with the sending and receiving devices synchronized.

Tardis   A device, once able to change shapes, that ended up frozen in the form of a British call-box in the Doctor Who television program. The term was coined by the character Susan Foreman in *Doctor Who and An Unearthly Child;* it stands for "Time And Relative Dimensions In Space."

TCP/IP (Transmission Control Protocol/Internet Protocol)   A set of protocols, resulting from ARPA efforts, used by the Internet to support services such as remote login (telnet), file transfer (FTP), and mail (SMTP).

telnet   The Internet standard protocol for remote terminal connection service. Telnet allows a user at one site to interact with a remote timesharing system at another site as if the user's terminal were connected directly to the remote computer.

terminal server   A small, specialized, networked computer that connects many terminals to a LAN through one network connection. Any user on the network can then connect to various network hosts.

TeX A free typesetting system by Donald Knuth.

TIA Thanks In Advance. Also, those who are very clever sometimes use the interesting form aTdHvAaNnKcSe.

twisted pair Cable made up of a pair of insulated copper wires wrapped around each other to cancel the effects of electrical noise.

UUCP (Unix to Unix Copy Program) A store-and-forward system, primarily for Unix systems but currently supported on other platforms (e.g., VMS and personal computers).

virus A program that "infects" other programs by embedding a copy of itself in them. (NHD)

Vote ACK Also known as a *Mass ACK*; in Usenet, the posting of the email address of each person that voted for or against a newsgroup proposal.

WAN (Wide-Area Network) A network spanning hundreds or thousands of miles.

workstation A networked personal computing device with more power than a standard IBM PC or Macintosh. Typically, a workstation has an operating system such as unix that is capable of running several tasks at the same time. It has several megabytes of memory and a large, high-resolution display. Examples are Sun workstations and Digital DECstations.

worm A computer program which replicates itself. The Internet worm (see page 93) was perhaps the most famous; it successfully (and accidentally) duplicated itself on many of the systems across the Internet.

wrt   With respect to.

veronica   A tool to search GopherSpace; also an acronym for "Very Easy Rodent-Oriented Net-wide Index to Computerized Archives."

zen   A Japanese sect of Buddhism that stresses attaining enlightenment through intuition rather than by studying scripture.

"*I hate definitions.*"

— Benjamin Disraeli, *Vivian Grey,*
bk i, chap ii

Bibliography

What follows is a compendium of sources with information that will be of use to anyone reading this guide. Most of them were used in the writing of the book, while others are simply noted because they are a must for any good net.citizen's bookshelf.

Books

Brunner, John (1975). *The Shockwave Rider.* Harper & Row: New York, NY.

Carl-Mitchell, Smoot and Quarterman, John S. (1993). *Practical Internetworking with TCP/IP and UNIX.* Addison-Wesley: Reading, MA.

Comer, Douglas E. (1991). *Internetworking With TCP/IP,* 3v. Prentice Hall: Englewood Cliffs, NJ.

Davidson, John (1988). *An Introduction to TCP/IP.* Springer-Verlag: Berlin.

Dern, Daniel P. (1994). *The Internet Guide for New Users.* McGraw-Hill: New York, NY.

Estrada, Susan (1993). *Connecting to the Internet.* O'Reilly and Associates: Sebastopol, CA.

Fisher, Sharon (1993). *Riding the Internet Highway.* New Riders Publishing: Carmel, IN.

Frey, Donnalyn and Adams, Rick (1993). *!@%:: A Directory of Electronic Mail Addressing and Networks.* O'Reilly and Associates: Sebastopol, CA.

Gibbs, Mark and Smith, Richard (1993). *Navigating the Internet.* Sams Publishing: Carmel, IN.

Gibson, William (1984). *Neuromancer.* Ace: New York, NY.

Hafner, Katie and Markoff, John (1991). *Cyberpunk: Outlaws and Hackers on the Computer Frontier.* Simon & Schuster: New York, NY.

Hiltz, Starr Roxanne and Turoff, Murray (1993). *The Network Nation: Human Communication via Computer, Revised Edition.* MIT Press: Cambridge, MA.

Krol, Ed (1992). *The Whole Internet User's Guide and Catalog.* O'Reilly and Associates: Sebastopol, CA.

LaQuey, Tracy and Ryer, Jeanne C. (1992). *The Internet Companion: A Beginner's Guide to Global Networking.* Addison-Wesley: Reading, MA.

LaQuey, Tracy (1990). *Users' Directory of Computer Networks.* Digital Press: Bedford, MA.

Levy, Stephen (1984). *Hackers: Heroes of the Computer Revolution.* Anchor Press/Doubleday: Garden City, NY.

Lynch, Daniel and Rose, Marshall, ed. (1993). *Internet System Handbook.* Addison-Wesley: Reading, MA.

Malamud, Carl (1992). *Exploring the Internet: A Technical Travelogue.* Prentice Hall: Englewood Cliffs, NJ.

Marine, April, et al. (1992). *Internet: Getting Started.* SRI International: Menlo Park, CA.

Partridge, Craig (1988). *Innovations in Internetworking.* ARTECH House: Norwood, MA.

Pirsig, Robert M. (1974). *Zen and the Art of Motorcycle Maintenance: An Inquiry into Values.* Morrow: New York, NY.

Rose, Marshall T. (1993). *The Internet Message: Closing the Book with Electronic Mail.* Prentice Hall: Englewood Cliffs, NJ.

Quarterman, John S. (1990). *The Matrix: Computer Networks and Conferencing Systems Worldwide.* Digital Press: Bedford, MA.

Raymond, Eric (ed) (1991). *The New Hacker's Dictionary.* MIT Press: Cambridge, MA.

Rittner, Don (1993). *Whole Earth Online Almanac.* Brady Publishing: New York, NY.

Stoll, Clifford (1989). *The Cuckoo's Egg.* Doubleday: New York, NY.

Tanenbaum, Andrew S. (1988). *Computer Networks, 2d ed.* Prentice-Hall: Englewood Cliffs, NJ.

Tennant, Roy, Ober, John and Lipow, Anne G., ed. (1993). *Crossing the Internet Threshold: An Instructional Handbook.* Library Solutions Press: Berkeley, CA.

Todino, Grace (1986). *Using UUCP and USENET: A Nutshell Handbook.* O'Reilly and Associates: Newton, MA.

The Waite Group (1991). *Unix Communications,* 2nd ed. Howard W. Sams & Company: Indianapolis, IN.

Periodicals, Papers, and Tapes

Arms, C. Using the National Networks: BITNET and the Internet. *Online* 14: 24-29.

Bailey, C.W. Electronic Publishing in Action: The Public Access Computer Systems Review and Other Electronic Serials. *Online* 15: 28-35.

Barlow, J. Coming Into The Country. *Communications of the ACM* 34:3 (March 1991): 2. Addresses "Cyberspace"—John Barlow was a co-founder of the EFF.

Bates, R., and White, K. *The KGB, the Computer, and Me.* Boston: WGBH for Nova, 1990. (58 min.) This documentary was based on *The Cuckoo's Egg.*

Catlett, C.E. The NSFNET: Beginnings of a National Research Internet. *Academic Computing* 3: 19-21, 59-64.

Cisler, S. NREN Update: More Meetings and New Tools. *Database* (April 1991): 96-98.

Collyer, G., and Spencer, H. News Need Not Be Slow. *Proceedings of the 1987 Winter USENIX Conference:* 181-90. USENIX Association, Berkeley, CA (January 1987).

Coursey, D. Riding the Internet: The Mystery of This Vast Collection of Networks. *Infoworld* (February 4, 1991).

Denning, P. The Internet Worm. *American Scientist* (March-April 1989): 126-128.

_____.The Science of Computing: Computer Networks. *American Scientist* (March-April 1985): 127-129.

Emtage, A., and Deutsch, P. *archie*—An Electronic Directory Service for the Internet. *Proceedings of the 1992 Winter USENIX Conference*: 93-110. USENIX Association, Berkeley, CA (January 1992).

Fisher, S. Whither NREN? *Byte* (July 1991): 181-190.

Frey, D., and Adams, R. USENET: Death by Success? *UNIX REVIEW* (August 1987): 55-60.

Ginsberg, K. Getting from Here to There. *UNIX REVIEW* (January 1986): 45.

Hiltz, S. R. The Human Element in Computerized Conferencing Systems. *Computer Networks* (December 1978): 421-428.

Horton, M. What is a Domain? *Proceedings of the Summer 1984 USENIX Conference*: 368-372. USENIX Association, Berkeley, CA (June 1984).

Jacobsen, Ole J. Information on TCP/IP. *ConneXions—The Interoperability Report* (July 1988): 14-15.

Jennings, D., et al. Computer Networking for Scientists. *Science* (28 February 1986): 943-950.

Jones, P. *What is the Internet?* Available on ftp.oit.unc.edu in 'pub/docs/whatis.internet'.

Krol, E. *The Hitchhiker's Guide to the Internet.* RFC-1118.

Lynch, C., and Preston, C. INTERNET access to information resources. Annual Review of Information Science and Technology (ARIST) (American Society for Information Science, vol 25): 263-311.

Markoff, J. "Author of computer 'virus' is son of U.S. electronic security expert". *New York Times* (Nov. 5, 1988): A1. Purists will notice the misuse of the term *virus*, rather than *worm*, in the title of the article.

_____."Computer snarl: A 'back door' ajar". *New York Times* (Nov. 7, 1988): B10.

Martin, J. *There's Gold in Them Thar Networks! or Searching for Treasure in All the Wrong Places.* FYI-10 and RFC-1290.

McQuillan, J. M., and Walden, D. C. The ARPA Network Design Decisions. *Computer Networks* (1977): 243-289.

Messmer, E. Internet Retrieval Tools Go On Market. *Network World* (Feb. 15, 1993): 29.

Ornstein, S. M. A letter concerning the Internet worm. *Communications of the ACM* 32:6 (June 1989).

Partridge, C. Mail Routing Using Domain Names: An Informal Tour. *Proceedings of the 1986 Summer USENIX Conference:* 366-76. USENIX Association, Berkeley, CA (June 1986).

Pethia, R., and van Wyk, K. *Computer Emergency Response—An International Problem.* Paper describing CERT and its origins. Available on cert.sei.cmu.edu in '/pub/doc'.

Polly, J. A. *Surfing the INTERNET: an Introduction.* Excellent and entertaining guide to the Net. *Surfing* is available on nysernet.org in the directory 'pub/resources/guides'.

Quarterman, J. Etiquette and Ethics. *ConneXions—The Interoperability Report* (March 1989): 12-16.

_____.Internet Misconceptions. *ComputerWorld* (Feb 22, 1993): 83.

_____.Notable Computer Networks. *Communications of the ACM* 29:10 (October 1986). This was the predecessor to *The Matrix*.

Raeder, A. W., and Andrews, K. L. Searching Library Catalogs on the Internet: A Survey. *Database* Searcher 6 (September 1990): 16-31.

Scientific American 265:3 (September 1991). This issue was dedicated to "Communications, Computers and Networks"; it contains articles addressing the past, present, and future of computer networking.

Seeley, D. A tour of the worm. *Proceedings of the 1989 Winter USENIX Conference:* 287-304. USENIX Association, Berkeley, CA (February 1989).

Shapiro, N., and Anderson, R. *Toward an Ethics and Etiquette for Electronic Mail.* Santa Monica, CA: RAND Corporation, Report R-3283-NSF/RC. Available on rand.org in 'pub/Reports'.

Shulman, G. Legal Research on USENET Liability Issues. *;login: The USENIX Association Newsletter* (December 1984): 11-17.

Smith, K. E-Mail to Anywhere. *PC World* (March 1988): 220-223.

Spafford, Eugene H. The Internet Worm: Crisis and Aftermath. *Communications of the ACM* 32:6 (June 1989): 678-687.

Stanton, D. *AARNet and the Academic Library. A Report on the Seminar/Workshop Held February 1992.* Murdoch, W.A.: Murdoch University Library. Available on csuvax1.csu.murdoch.edu.au in 'pub/library' as 'newcwkshp.rpt'.

Stoll, C. Stalking the Wily Hacker. *Communications of the ACM* 31:5 (May 1988): 484-497. This article grew into the book *The Cuckoo's Egg.*

Taylor, D. The Postman Always Rings Twice: Electronic Mail in a Highly Distributed Environment. *Proceedings of the 1988 Winter USENIX Conference:* 145-153. USENIX Association, Berkeley, CA (December 1988).

U.S. Gen'l Accounting Ofc. Computer Security: Virus Highlights Need for Improved Internet Management. *GAO/ IMTEC* -89 - 57, (1989). Addresses the Internet worm .

Wright, Robert. Voice of America: Overhearing the Internet. *The New Republic* (September 13, 1993): 20-27.

"All the rest is mere fine writing".

— Paul Verlaine, *Art poetique,* 1882.

Index

A

ACM, 97
Adams, Rick, 42
address
    email, 9
    Internet (IP), 4
administrivia, 15, 168
agriculture, 65, 69
aliens, 64
America Online, 127
ANSI, 168
AppleLink, 127
archie, 29
    and Bunyip, 89
archive server, 133
ATTmail, 128

B

backbone
    Internet, 6
    Usenet, 38
bang path, 10

basketweaving, 50
Barlow, John Perry, xiii
Barron, Billy, 60
BBS, 70
bible, 79
BITFTP, 134
BITNET, 6, 16
BIX
    connecting to, 91
    sending email to, 128
buddhism, 180
Bunyip Info Svcs, 89

C

CARL, 63
ClariNet, 88
Clinton, Bill, 106
CMC, 122
compressed files, 29
CompuServe
    connecting to, 91
    sending email to, 128
CPSR, 98
cross-posting, 50

Cyberspace, xv, xvii, 93, 104
Cygnus Support, 102

D

databases
    agriculture, 65, 69
    archie, 29
    extragalactic, 64
    general info, 66
    jobs, 70, 114
    library, 63, 68
    marine studies, 68
    physics, 91
    scholarships, 64
    space, 67
    whatis, 33
    WHOIS, 84
December, John, 122
Dern, Daniel, 118
domains, 2

E

earthquakes, 76
EFF, 100
electronic journals, 87
email
    addresses, 9
    bounced, 10
    posting to Usenet, 48

F

FidoNet, 129
finding friends, 83
finger, 75
FQDN, 3
freenet, 61
FSF, 101
FYI, 122

G

gambling, 176
GEnie
    connecting to, 92
    sending email to, 129
geographic server, 65
Gore, Al
    contacting, 106
    and NREN, 111
GNU Project, 101
gopher, 80
government, 106

H

ham radio, 66
headers, 11
hytelnet, 60

I

Info Scout, 75, 105
Internet address, 4
Internet Society, 102
Internet Talk Radio, 112
Internet worm, 93
InterNIC, 105, 120
IP address, 4

J

jobs, 70, 114
journals, electronic, 87

K

Kamens, Jonathan, 54
knowbot, 62
Kovacs, Diane, 87

L

Larsen, Ron, 59
leased line, 6
libraries, 59, 63
Library of Congress, 67
listserv, 16
    retrieval, 87
LPF, 103

M

MaasInfo, 121
magazines, 119
mailing lists, 15
Malamud, Carl, 112
mathematics, 63
MCImail, 130
Morrison, Jim, 10
MTV, 107

N

Nass, Simona, 104
netfind, 83
netmailsites, 68
news, reading, 39
NIST, 72
NNTP, 45, 175
NREN, 111
NTP, 175

O

Online Career Center, 114
Oracle, Usenet, 18

P

ping, 77
Postel, Jon, 122

postmaster, 12
Power, Matt, 86
Prodigy, 131
Project Gutenberg, 108

Q

Quarterman, John, 117, 119

R

resolving, 4
RFC, 122
    FYIs, 122
Rickard, Jack, 119

S

scholarships, 64
Schwartz, Michael, 83
Scott, Peter, 60
SEA, 103
security
    with finger, 76
    with ftp, 24
    BBS, 152
signature files, 47
SLIP, 6
space, 67
Spafford, Gene, 16
St. George, Art, 59
Stallman, Richard, 101

Stephenson, Neal, 118
Stoll, Cliff, 97
Strangelove, Michael, 87
stupid joke, 19, 50, 176
subnet, 4

T

talk, 78

U

Usenet, 35
    reading news, 39
    Oracle, 18
UUCP, 5
    bang paths, 10
    mail handling, 10
    and Usenet, 38

V

veronica, 82

W

WAIS, 79
Waldo, 53
weather, 70
    at MIT, 76
whatis, 33

White House, 106
White Pages, 62
whois, 84

Y

Yanoff, Scott, 60

Z

Z file extension, 29